YOU CAN PLAY TENNIS

This comprehensive handbook has been specially designed for beginners and those wishing to improve their tennis technique by one of Britain's foremost tennis players.

Basic strokes, practice routines, tactical play and hundreds of inside tips and hints on making the most of your game and a dazzling impact on the courts of this fast-paced, exciting sport.

Also published by CAROUSEL BOOKS

YOU CAN BE A GYMNAST
YOU CAN PLAY FOOTBALL
YOU CAN PLAY CRICKET
YOU CAN SWIM
YOU CAN RIDE

YOU CAN PLAY TENNIS

A CAROUSEL BOOKS 0 552 54241 5

First published in Great Britain by Carousel Books

PRINTING HISTORY
Carousel edition published 1983

Carousel Books are published by
Transworld Publishers Ltd.,
Century House, 61–63 Uxbridge Road,
Ealing, London W5 5SA

Made and printed in Great Britain by the
Guernsey Press Co. Ltd., Guernsey, Channel Islands.

You Can Play Tennis

with
David Lloyd

Illustrated by Mike Miller

CAROUSEL BOOKS
A DIVISION OF TRANSWORLD PUBLISHERS LTD.

CONTENTS

A WORD FROM DAVID LLOYD . . .

You **can** play tennis — everybody can play tennis, and it is one of the best sports to enjoy. In the past people have felt that they had to have reached a certain standard before they dared approach the courts and Clubs. Those days have gone. Tennis, as a sport, is about to undergo a boom in popularity in Britain, parallel to that experienced over the last ten years in North America and Europe. That boom has been initiated by the discovery that tennis is fun at all sorts of levels: it is good for you, and it can increasingly be played all the year round in comfortable and sociable conditions.

Leisure centres offering tennis, and modern, purpose-built indoor tennis clubs are beginning to mushroom in Britain, encouraged by this rapidly growing interest. There has been a break-through in the discovery of modern, all-weather surfaces for year-round play.

Tennis, then, can mean enjoyment and health to anyone, but it can also offer a very well-paid career to a talented and dedicated few; a quite spectacular career, with an earning potential that can scarcely be matched in any other field. Why not start? It's never too late, or too early, to learn, and you start right here.

This book outlines a simple and basic approach to the game of tennis. It's entirely suitable for someone tackling the game for the first time, or as guide to those faced with introducing beginners to the game. Each individual stroke has been painstakingly described for ease of interpretation. Tactics, scoring, doubles play, it is all here.

The idea of teaching 'Short Tennis' as a preliminary to the larger game is extremely sound, particularly for very young players. From a very early age, children can cope with the shorter racket and soft ball, and this aids enjoyment from the start, while developing skills which will be invaluable later. Adults too can benefit from this approach, especially if they are totally new to racket games.

I believe too that an enormous benefit can be gained for a beginner by using a practice wall to help groove ground strokes. This can start against the garage or the garden shed, and will be found to be time well spent when you finally reach the court.

Don't be discouraged, however, if you feel that your style is less than perfect, when you compare it to that described in the book. Few **top** players have an entirely orthodox approach. Never forget that the game begins and ends with your ability to get the ball over the net, and in play. The instructions in this book demonstrate the best and most straightforward way to do that, but it's easy to become bogged down in technique and forget that one basic requirement. **You** can play tennis. Start here and now, and share some of the enjoyment that the game has given me.

David Lloyd

THE HISTORY OF TENNIS

For the sake of accuracy, and to get the matter over and done with, let's get the name of the game sorted out. Although the subject of this book is known throughout the world as simply 'tennis', strictly speaking the correct name is **Lawn Tennis**. However, the governing body of the game throughout the world is called the **International Tennis Federation** (I.T.F.).

Why call it Lawn Tennis, you may ask? After all, much of the playing in the world today takes place on clay courts or hard courts. The answer is that lawn tennis developed out of a much older game as recently as the middle of the nineteenth century. That older game is still played, though on a greatly reduced scale from its heyday three hundred years ago. It is called **Real** (or **Royal**) **Tennis** and it's worth spending a little time looking at it, for in it you will see many of the features of the game that thrills so many millions of people every summer during the U.S., French, Australian and Wimbledon lawn tennis championships.

There is nothing particularly new about hitting a ball with your hand or some sort of bat or racket. The Egyptians, the ancient Greeks, the Romans, the Persians, the Mexicans and the Saracens all played ball games of some sort, and the modern word 'racket' comes from the Arabic word for the palm of the hand.

By the eleventh century *le jeu de paume* had become popular in France.

The game probably began in the open but it reached its popularity in monastery cloisters where the monks hit a ball around the quadrangles and sloping roofs that surrounded them.

Le jeu de paume literally means the game of the palm, and at first the ball was hit with the palm of the hand. As it developed, gloves, wooden bats, wooden frames covered with parchment, like tambourines, and finally **rackets** were used.

From these early rackets, which first appeared about five hundred years ago, every modern racket has developed.

The game became truly Royal Tennis at about this time too. Successive kings of France were devoted to the sport and where they led their nobles followed. By 1600 tennis had become a national pastime in France. There were 1,800 courts in Paris alone, according to one visitor, and though most of these would have been outdoor courts for the game that had developed outside (*longue paume*), there were probably 250 indoor courts for the playing of real tennis, as it survives today.

You can see one of these indoor courts at Hampton Court palace, which belonged to Henry VIII, who was a very keen player, and there are more recent courts in other parts of Great Britain, Australia and North America. These courts look very like the monastery quadrangles where the first games were played. The hard floor is surrounded by four walls, three of which have roofs that slope down into the court. These represent the roofs of the cloisters in the monasteries and they form an important part of the playing area of the court. (Real tennis is a game which involves the use of the walls as well as the floor area.) Other features of monastery architecture are preserved in real tennis courts to add diversity to the game. There is a buttress at one end, a door and galleries, all of which add to the variety of shots that can be played.

From its great popularity in the fifteenth and sixteenth centuries real tennis fell into decline and by the late eighteenth century only a few courts remained open. The game had become restricted to the aristocracy, where once it had been enjoyed by people from every walk of life. A revival took place in the nineteenth century, particularly in England, but it was still a game for the privileged few. With a growing national interest in outdoor games, though, there was a growing need for a popular game that could be played by all.

Various forms of outdoor tennis were played from the mid-nineteenth century onwards. The first lawn tennis club was formed in Leamington Spa in 1872 but it was a year later that a game called **Sphairistiké** literally set the ball rolling. This was devised by Major Walter Wingfield. He designed the game to be played on grass (though he added that it could be played on ice as well).

The court was shaped like an hour-glass, bulging at each end with a narrow 'waist' at the middle. This waist was spanned by a net 6.4m long, 1.52m high at each end and 1.42m high at the centre. It looked more like the net in real tennis than the familiar lawn tennis net.

'**Sticky**', as the game was nicknamed, was not the overwhelming success that its inventor might have wished for, but its popularity was sufficient to interest the Victorian public in the possibilities of adapting real tennis to a game that could be played in gardens by both men and women, with the minimum amount of equipment. Two years after 'sticky' first appeared, the **All England Croquet Club** made available one of its grounds for the sole purpose of playing lawn tennis, which indicates how popular the game had become. As yet there were no fixed rules. There were disagreements about the shape of the court, the height of the net, the method of serving and the position of the serving line.

Before holding the first lawn tennis championships the All England Croquet and Lawn Tennis Club, to which the former club changed its name in April 1877, decided to set out the rules for the competition. Henry Jones was appointed as the referee and with a committee of two other men he drafted a new set of rules which have been the basis of lawn tennis ever since. This little committee changed the shape of the court from Major Wingfield's hourglass to the rectangular court with measurements very like those still in use. It also introduced a new scoring system to replace the one from the game of rackets, which had previously been used in other forms of lawn tennis.

The first championships were held at **Wimbledon** early in July 1877. Twenty-two competitors took part, the winner being **Spencer Gore**, who became the first Wimbledon champion. His success was due largely to his skill at volleying his opponents high returns, that is hitting them before they bounced.

Many players used to playing either real tennis or rackets, both of which require techniques different to those needed for lawn tennis, had difficulty in changing to the new game. Many of the early matches were dominated by strong services and many of the rallies were careful exchanges across the net from the baseline.

In the 1878 competition, the **overarm service** appeared for the first time and in the final, Gore was defeated by **Hadow**, whose delicate lobs over Gore's head wore him out as he dashed from the net to the back of the court to retrieve the returns.

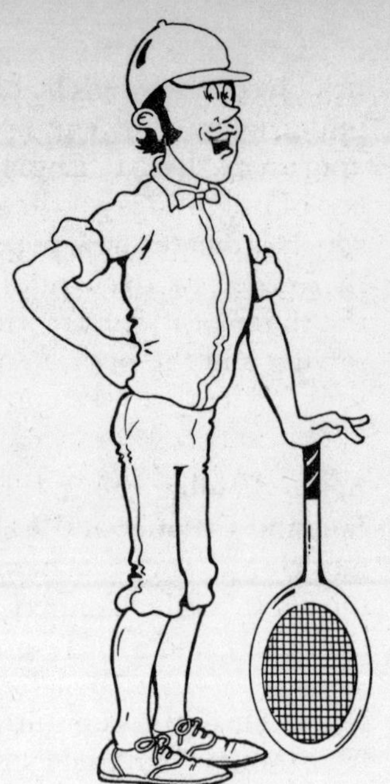

The first real lawn tennis players, the ones to show a distinct flair for the new game by hitting the ball hard and flat, smashing and volleying determinedly to unsettle their opponents, were two brothers, **Ernest** and **William Renshaw**. They brought the first thrills and excitement to Wimbledon creating a public interest that has been growing ever since. There were 200 spectators for the first championship but only eight years later, when William Renshaw played Lawford in the final in 1885 there were 3,500 people to watch that match alone.

In 1882 the governing bodies of the game decided to lower the net, a move which encouraged **ground stroke** play and took away some of the advantage that the volleyers had enjoyed. In 1879 the first men's doubles competition had been held in Oxford and in the same year, the first lawn tennis competition for women had been held in Ireland. Mixed doubles followed 9 years later in 1888.

Meanwhile lawn tennis had spread far and wide. The **United States Lawn Tennis Association** (USLTA) was founded in 1881, when the first US men's singles competition was held, to be followed in 1887 by the first U.S. women's championship. Similar competitions had been established in Australia, France and Germany by the end of the century.

The first international lawn tennis match was played between England and Ireland in 1892.

In 1900, the first **Davis Cup** match was played between Britain and the U.S.A. in Boston — the Americans won 3–0. Today over 50 countries compete in the Davis Cup.

In 1923, the **Wightman Cup** competition was staged for the first time between women players from Britain and the U.S.A.. (Women had first played at Wimbledon in 1884 when the champion was Maud Watson.)

In 1913, the **ITF** was formed in Paris to take over control of the sport worldwide and this was one of the chief opponents of the move to open competitions, that is to allow professionals and amateurs to play against each other. Even in its early days, the popularity of tennis was such that the best players could earn very large sums for playing exhibition matches. The great French women's champion, **Suzanne Lenglen**, who won the women's title at Wimbledon six times and ruled the women's game in the 1920's, reputedly turned professional for a fee of $100,000, which gives some idea of the fortunes that awaited the best players.

This distinction between amateurs and professionals kept many of the leading players out of major competitions until 1968 when the first open tournament was played in England. This was followed that summer by the first open Wimbledon, won by **Rod Laver**, who the following year completed the first open **grand slam** (winning the four major titles, the Australian, French, U.S. and Wimbledon men's singles). He had previously completed the grand slam as an amateur in 1962, but at that time many of the best competitors were barred from playing against him because they were professionals.

Other changes have come about in the 1970's. Tennis players have joined the ranks of footballers, boxers and golfers as being superstars in the eyes of their public. Huge sums of money are now won by the top players and the competition at the top is fiercer than it has ever been. The European players are starting to make something of a comeback after the domination by American and Australian players. Sweden, Czechoslovakia and France are producing promising young players, the most famous of which is undoubtedly the remarkable **Bjorn Borg**. British players, too, have achieved some notable international successes which point to a steady improvement in the national game.

With this intense pressure, the age of many of the competitors, especially among the women seems to fall each year; **Kathy Rinaldi** (USA) was still 14 when she played at Wimbledon in 1981 and **Andrea Jaeger** was seeded in 1980 when she was only 19 days over her 15th birthday. For the youngest champion, you have to look back almost 100 years, however, to 1887 when **Charlotte Dod** took the women's singles title at the age of 15 years 9 months. Mind you, things were different in those days, with only a handful of players to compete against!

TOURNAMENTS AND COMPETITIONS

Competitive lawn tennis is divided into tournaments where players compete as individuals and team competitions like the **Davis Cup** or the **Federation Cup**.

Dealing with tournaments first, there are four major champoinships known as the '**grand slam**' – Wimbledon; Paris (France); Flushing Meadow (USA) and Australia. The U.S. Championships, date back to 1881. The French championships began ten years later, and have always been regarded as the major clay court event. And the first national event was held in Australia in 1905.

The top players in these and other major competitions are **seeded**, which means that they are placed in protected positions in the draw to avoid them meeting early in the competition and this seeding is done according to the order given by the **ATP** (Association of Tennis Professionals) computer ranking list.

In the international team competitions, the **Davis Cup** is the oldest. This was presented by Dwight F. Davis, a leading American player in 1900. The form of the competition is the same today as it was at the start of the century. Each team has a maximum of four players, with the option of having an additional non-playing captain, who sits by the umpire's chair encouraging his players. The competition lasts over three days with two singles matches on the first day, a doubles on the second day and two reverse singles on the third day. (In the reverse singles the players on the first day change opponents.) Until 1972, the holder of the Davis Cup took no part in the competition until the 'challenge round'. As the competition spread and as more nations competed the number of games increased and it became necessary to hold zone and inter-zone finals in the early stages of the competition. In the end, the Davis Cup was spread over nearly half the year to accomodate all the preliminary stages that came before the 'challenge round'. But in 1972, the challenge round was abolished leaving the holder nation to play its way through to the zone final before competing in the final of the competition proper. Two nations, Australia and the U.S.A. have dominated the Davis Cup; in the 18 years between 1950 and 1967, Australian teams won the Davis Cup 15 times!

The **Federation Cup** is the international lawn tennis competition for women. This was inaugurated in 1963 to mark the 50th anniversary of the International Lawn Tennis

Federation. Unlike the Davis Cup, the tournament takes place in one centre each year, with the host nation changing from one year to the next. Each team consists of not more than three players, and matches are decided on the outcome of two singles matches and one doubles. As with the Davis Cup, the two principal nations have been Australia and the U.S.A. although European countries, notably West Germany, Britain and the Netherlands have all reached the final, and the 1972 competition was won by the host nation South Africa.

The **Wightman Cup**, like the Davis Cup was presented by and is named after a leading American tennis player; in this case Mrs. Hazel Hotchkiss Wightman. Mrs. Wightman was one of the greatest American tennis players of all time winning her first U.S. title in 1909 and her last in 1943! The competition which bears her name is played every year between teams from the USA and Britain. This a private match between the two countries held alternately in Britain and America. The teams consist of three singles players and two doubles pairs, requiring a minimum of four players on each side. The match consists of two doubles matches and five singles matches and takes place over three days.

The American team won the first Wightman Cup competition in 1923 and although the British won the following year, the competition has been dominated by the Americans, though in recent years the British have provided increasingly stiffer opposition.

The leading international indoor competition for men is the **King's Cup**, more correctly called the King of Sweden's Cup, which has been supported by the Swedish royal family since it began in 1936. Although there is nothing to prevent nations outside Europe taking part, most of the competitors have been European countries. The matches are played on wooden or plastic indoor courts in November and December each year. Many national tennis organizations look on the King's Cup as a very important tournament for giving young players a taste of international competition before the Davis Cup, and the King's Cup also provides useful practice against top-class competition during the winter months.

With all this discussion of international competitions and leading world tournaments you may wonder what the beginner has to aim for. At the back of the book you will find full details of a very good way of gaining experience in tennis and winning your first award. This is the **Lawn Tennis Performance Award Scheme**. It may not be as tough as winning a Wimbledon singles final, but to the successful candidates it is just as rewarding, just as useful, just as important, and it may set you on the path to the Wimbledon title.

THE TENNIS COURT

All kinds of surfaces are used for playing tennis today. The fastest is still the **grass** surface of traditional lawn tennis. But the game is played on many man-made surfaces like **asphalt** and **concrete**, as well as **clay**, **sand** and **gravel**. While indoors it is played on **rubber**, **plastic**, **nylon** and **wooden** surfaces; the fastest of these being wood.

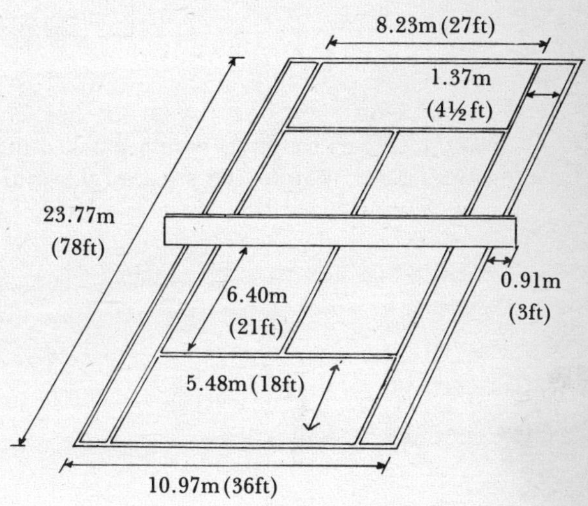

The lawn tennis court can be used for either **singles** games between two players, or **doubles** games between two pairs of players. The singles game is played in an area 23.77m long by 8.23m wide and the doubles game is played in an area that is also 23.77m long but 10.97m wide. The two areas that run down either side of the court are known as '**tramlines**' or '**alleys**'.

A lawn tennis court is marked out by **lines**. All of these lines form part of the playing area, which means that even if a shot touches the outside edge of a line it is still regarded as being **'in court'**.

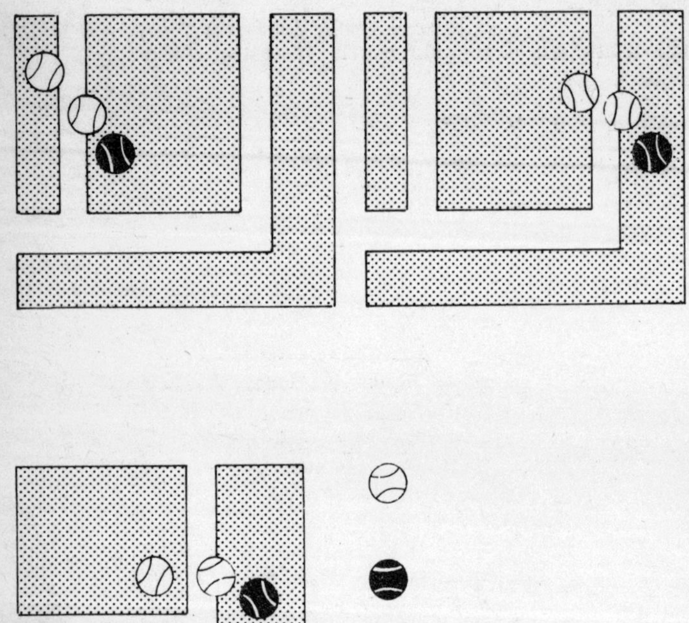

Only when the ball lands beyond the outer limit of one of these lines is it judged to be **'out of court'**.

The tennis **court** (as it is usually called) is divided in half by a **net** 1.07m high at the posts and 0.914m high at the centre. This net is suspended by a wire attached to the posts and can be adjusted to raise or lower its height. The posts are set 0.914m from the sidelines, which vary, of course, depending on whether you are playing a singles or a doubles game.

If you play a singles game on a court with net posts in the position for a doubles game, you should place singles sticks 0.914m out from the sidelines to mark where the posts should be.

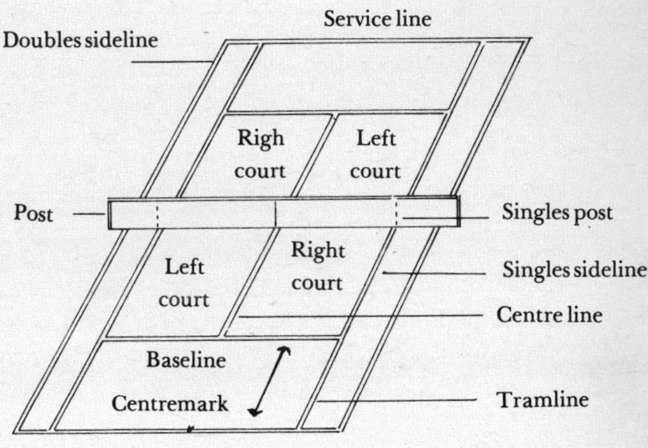

THE GAME

The object of tennis, like that of most games, is to win a match. Matches are made up of a certain number of **sets**, which are made up of a certain number of **games** which are each formed from **points**. In leading men's competitions the winner is decided on the best of **five** sets; in other competition and all ladies' tournaments the best of **three** sets basis applies.

Tennis is a game of skill, speed and fast reactions. At all levels it is a game won or lost by ball control. Since most points are won through opponents making mistakes, the better your own ball control, the fewer mistakes you are likely to make. In the same way if you have good ball control, you will be more successful in playing the ball in a way which will force your opponents to make mistakes.

A match is started by spinning a racket or tossing a coin. The winner of the spin or toss can then decide whether to serve or whether to receive, or which end to begin playing at. Alternatively he or she can ask the opponent to make the choices.

Once each player is in position, there is a warm-up period of four minutes when they knock balls across the net to each other going through each of their strokes and getting a feel for the court. After the warm-up, the first game of the match begins.

The **server** always starts from the **right** court. He or she must stand behind the baseline between the centre mark and the sideline, making sure not to touch the baseline with his or her feet until the ball has been hit. The server throws the ball into the air with one hand and strikes it so that it passes over the net without bouncing and lands in the service court diagonally opposite.

The server has two chances to serve (first service and second service). If both serves fail, the server loses the point.

The **receiver** may stand anywhere on his or her side of the net to make a return stroke. The served ball must be hit before it makes its second bounce, but it may **not** be hit before it touches the ground (volleyed).

Once the ball has been returned a **rally** begins in which the players hit the ball over the net, trying to play it so that their opponent is forced to make a mistake. A player loses a point by hitting the ball **out of court**; by hitting it **into the net** so that it fails to land on the other side; by letting the ball **bounce twice**; and by serving a **double fault**, as mentioned above. A player can also lose by a point by **hitting a ball twice**. This usually happens by accident.

Once the first point has been decided, the server moves to the **left** court and serves from there into the service court diagonally opposite, as before. The server continues to serve from alternate boxes until the game is completed.

At the start of the second game, the server becomes the receiver and the receiver becomes the server. The players then alternate the service in this way throughout the match.

The procedure is very much the same in a doubles match. After the toss, the serving team decides which of them will serve first and the other pair decide who will serve in the second game. (The third server partners the first server and the fourth server partners the second server.) The receivers decide in which part of the court they wish to receive service for their first receiving game and cannot exchange receiving courts until a set has been played. In the same way the order of serving can be changed at the start of a new set.

SCORING

It isn't necessary to go into all the detailed rules of lawn tennis at this stage. If you want to study the rules, you will find a complete copy in your local library or at the nearest tennis club.

It is, however, important to understand how to score in tennis and since this is unlike scoring in most other games, it's worth outlining in detail. It will also help you understand the mounting excitement of matches that you watch on television or anywhere else.

While a game is being played, the server's score is always given **first** to avoid confusion; so a score given as '40 – 15' tells you that the server is in the lead by 2 points. In tennis four points in a row wins the game. These are the points:

1st point — 15

2nd point — 30

3rd point — 40

4th point — Game

When no points are scored, the expression used is '**love**', i.e. '40 — love', which means 3 points to nil in favour of the server.

If both players score 3 points the score becomes 40–40. This is called **deuce** and at this point one of the players must win 2 points in a row to win the game. The first point won after deuce is given as advantage to that player; if he or she wins the next point, the game is one. If the opponent wins the point after advantage however, the score returns to deuce again. Some of the most exciting tennis takes place in games in which advantage switches from one player or pair to the other several times before the winning shot is made.

To win a set, a player or pair must win 6 games. If the score reaches 5 – 5, 'five all' a player or pair must win two games in a row, to win the set 7 – 5. This is known as an **advantage** set.

If the score reaches 6–6 'six all' the **tie-break** scoring system comes into operation. This avoids long, drawn-out sets. The tie-break is used in all but the final sets of a match, though in some indoor matches and certain tournaments it is also used in the final sets. The tie-break is won by the first player or pair to win 7 points provided that there is a winning margin of 2 points (from 7–0 to 7–5). Should the score reach 6–6 the tie-break carries on until one of the players or pairs wins 2 points in a row. During the tie break, the players or pairs serve alternately for 2 consecutive points, with the first point being played from the right court. The players change ends after every six points and at the end of the tie-break game.

As mentioned earlier, matches are played over the best of either five or three sets. In a five-set match, the first player to win three sets is the winner. In a three-set match, the first player to win two sets is the winner. The magic words that announce victory or defeat come at the end of the final point when the umpire announces, *'Game, set and match to . . .'*.

EQUIPMENT AND CLOTHING

You may think that equipping yourself for tennis is just a matter of buying the racket that looks the nicest, picking up a couple of balls, putting on a pair of shoes and going off to find somewhere to play. It can be like that, of course, but you will do your tennis no good in the long run if you don't take some care, particularly in how you choose your racket.

Tennis rackets are made in different sizes and weights and have different sized grips. It is important when choosing your first racket to make sure that it suits **you**.

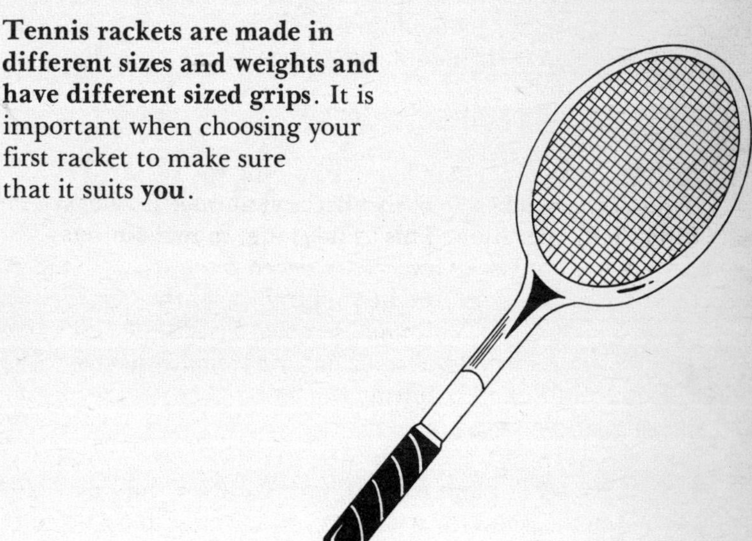

Don't go for the most expensive or the one you like the look of best, just for the sake of it. Take care in trying different rackets for size before making your choice. Although steel, aluminium and other materials are used for tennis rackets, wooden ones are still hard to beat and they are certainly the best bet for beginners.

Most of the leading manufacturers make junior rackets for young players. These are smaller and lighter than full-sized rackets and they have smaller grips too. When your game progresses you can change to light, light-medium, or medium rackets, but you will gain nothing by using a racket that is too big for you, and it could put you off the game altogether.

When trying out your racket, check the grip by wrapping your hand round the handle and seeing where your thumb is in relation to your second finger nail. It should not overlap it. If it does, the grip is too small.

Then try holding the racket away from you and see how it feels. The racket should feel evenly balanced though slightly light towards the head. Remember that it will feel heavier on court when you are hitting the ball.

One other point to bear in mind when you buy your racket is the **stringing**. While most tournament players will want 'gut' stringing, beginners are much better off with synthetic stringing. This lasts longer and is cheaper than gut.

There are two main types of **grip covering**, leather and towelling. Whichever you prefer, it should be kept in good condition and it will require replacing from time to time.

Tennis balls are made to conform to strict standards of size and bounce, and though it is tempting to buy cheap balls, these really are a false economy. Once a ball starts to lose its bounce or covering, the way it behaves changes considerably. So it's important, particularly when you are beginning, to play with proper balls and rackets, to use the best balls you can. These will help you master the proper techniques by behaving in a conventional way. If you learn to play with balls that bounce very little, for example, you will have great difficulty to adjusting your game to balls that bounce in a normal way.

Ideally you should have half a dozen balls to use when you are playing, though you can make do with four. The more balls you have, the less chasing around you will have to do during your games.

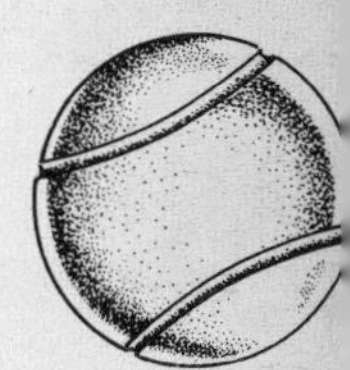

Two other useful items of equipment are a **racket press**

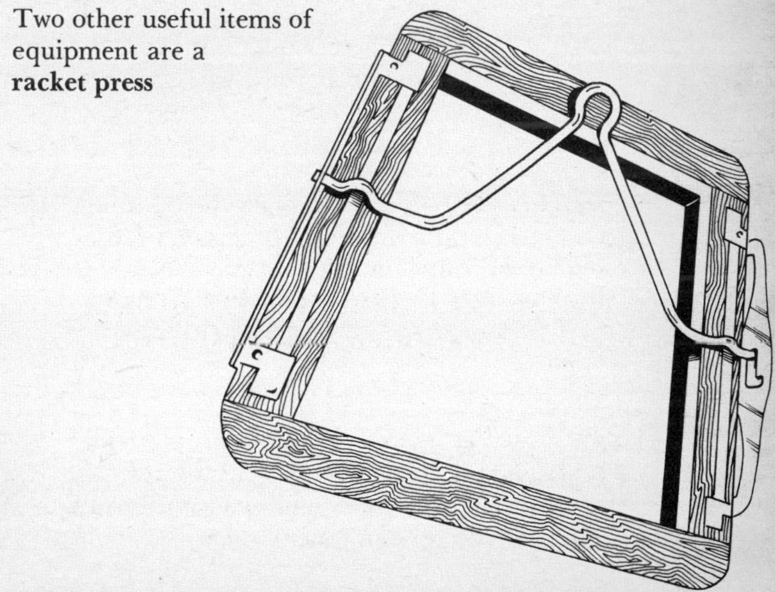

and a **racket headcover**.

The press will help your racket keep its shape when it is not in use and the headcover protects it while you are travelling to or from a game.

When it comes to **clothes** to wear for tennis the important point to bear in mind is that they must not be too tight, so restricting your movement.

The usual tennis clothing for men is shorts and a short-sleeved shirts while women wear skirts and a top or tennis dresses. These clothes are usually white and many tennis clubs insist on their players wearing 'whites'.

In cold weather, tracksuits can be worn because your muscles need to be warm and loose for tennis.

Tennis shoes should not be too tight either. They should be comfortable with good arch support. Socks with cushioned soles will give the best protection to your feet as well.

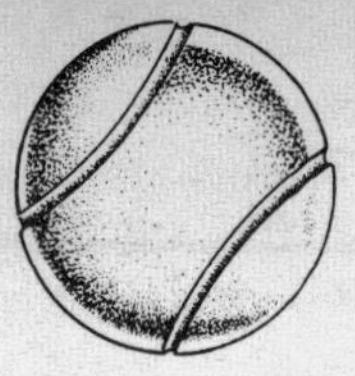

GETTING STARTED — BALL SENSE

As has already been mentioned, a game of tennis can be lost or won by ball sense. Obviously this is important, but what exactly is it? In tennis, the biggest challenge is getting to the right place at the right time so that you can be properly balanced and ready to return a ball that has been played by your opponent, who wants to make it as difficult for you as possible.

> Judging the speed of the ball, judging its flight, knowing the best position to be in to play it and being able to move quickly and efficiently — all this is ball sense.

Don't worry if it sounds complicated. To most of us it is a natural, automatic response. You can judge how good your ball sense is in a few, simple exercises. These don't require anything more than a tennis ball, and it doesn't have to be a new one. And remember, ball sense isn't limited to tennis, it's a skill used in football, cricket, hockey, or any other ball game. Remember also that it is a skill that can be developed with practice, so don't give up if you find your ball sense isn't all that it might be at first.

In practising and developing ball sense for tennis you want to bear two requirements in mind. These are the ways in which you will **receive** the ball.

The ball will come to you in two ways depending on the sort of stroke you play. Balls coming to you **after** they have bounced once are played with groundstrokes. These have two flights — the first flight before the bounce, the second after. Balls hit before they bounce have only one flight.

Therefore, in your practice you want to get used to dealing with balls that come straight to you without bouncing and with those that bounce once. (If there is spin on the ball, it will change direction after it bounces, so you need to get used to anticipating spin too.)

BALL SENSE EXERCISES

1. Start with catching exercises.

I don't say 'simple catching exercises' because, easy as these may be to you, they still require concentration. The fact that they are easy does not mean that you should let your eyes off the ball. This concentration is vital with easy tennis shots too. Many players throw away points by failing to concentrate on shots because they think they are easy and play loose or inaccurate strokes as a result.

With a partner, throw a ball to each other at different speeds and heights. Start by catching with both hands, trying not to drop any of the catches. When you are catching the ball every time, try catching it with one hand, and then using each hand in turn. Practise without bouncing the ball at first.

2. Now introduce the bounce.

Throw the ball as before, but bouncing it before it reaches your partner. Start by catching with both hands just after the top of the balls bounce. **Vary your throws**. Throw some short, so that your partner has to run in to catch them before the ball bounces twice.

Throw some long so that he or she has to run back to catch the ball. Throw the ball on one side or the other, making your partner move to the side to catch it.

Try to make your throws as varied and unexpected as possible, without making them impossibly hard for your partner to catch. At this stage the idea is to practise, not to beat your opponent. Then catch the ball with one hand and finally using each hand in turn. Remember that you are trying to catch the ball **just after the top of its bounce** – this is the way you will want to play every groundstroke.

3. Try playing both games (no-bounce and bounce) with two balls.

Start with one each and throw them to each other when one of you calls 'Throw'. Take turns in calling.

4. Using targets.

When you have both become confident at catching bouncing balls, play a game using targets on which you must aim to bounce the ball, but throw it in a way that will make it difficult for your partner to catch. Start with a big target, say a paper circle pinned to the ground, but as you become more accurate make the target smaller, ending up with a coin. Score 3 points for a hit on the target and lose 1 for a dropped catch. The first player to reach 30 wins. Catch with both hands or one-handed.

You might want to practise on your own, if there is no one to partner you, and you can do this perfectly well against a wall, though watch out for the windows if they are too close!

1. Start by throwing the ball against the wall and catching it two-handed before it bounces. Throw it gently at first and increase the speed as you get better.

2. Do the same but catch the ball with one hand, and then each hand in turn.

3. Repeat this exercise but turn round before catching the ball.

4. Place a target in front of the wall (a large target to begin with) and bounce the ball on this before it hits the wall, catch it on the rebound. Start by standing in front of the target, so that the ball comes directly back to you, but when you are more confident, angle your throws, so that the ball rebounds away from you, making you run across to catch it. Start catching with two hands and then move to one-handed catching.

These exercises are just guidelines. You can have fun inventing your own games. Do remember the principles behind the games, though. You want to practise moving quickly and easily to the ball. You want to learn to catch it cleanly. You want to get used to catching the ball just after the top of its bounce. And above all else you want to train your eyes to concentrate on the ball the whole time.

GETTING USED TO THE RACKET

Today many young beginners start to play tennis with the game called **Short Tennis**. This is similar to tennis but it is played with a foam rubber ball and short bats, and it usually takes place indoors on a badminton court. Short Tennis is a very useful way of gaining experience of applying your ball sense to hitting a moving ball with a bat or racket. The Short Tennis ball moves slower than a proper tennis ball, which makes it easier to hit. The Short Tennis bat is easier to use than a tennis racket too. The result is that beginners quickly develop enough skill to play enjoyable rallies and in doing this they learn many of the basic skills of positioning and playing the ball over the net. If you have a chance, try to make your first game of tennis a Short Tennis game, you'll enjoy it and it will help your progress. Whether you use a Short Tennis bat or a junior tennis racket, there are exercises you can practise to help your racket control and help you apply your ball sense. Before you even start to hit a tennis ball with your racket, though, you need to know how to hold it — and the way you hold the racket is known as the **grip**.

GRIPS

You will hear a lot of talk about the advantages and disadvantages of different grips. You will probably notice many leading players using a variety of grips. While it's true to say that there are a number of different grips used, most of these have developed out of the basic grips used for sound, simple hitting. As you progress as a player, you may feel the need to alter your grip to give yourself the best chance of using your skill to the utmost. When you start, though, concentrate on the three basic grips, shown here. Once you have mastered these, you may have no need to change later on. If you do feel a need, ask a professional coach to help you. Whatever you do, don't decide on a particular grip at random, or because your particular tennis hero or heroine uses it. They use it because it suits them, but there is no guarantee that it will suit you. Using the wrong grip could limit your game considerably. That's why it is important to learn the basic grips from the outset.

FOREHAND GRIP — drives and volleys

Most players use a grip called '**Eastern**' or '**shake hands**' grip as the palm of the hand is behind the handle and this makes it stronger and easier to hit all kinds of balls.

The grip gets its name ('Eastern') because it was first used on the clay courts of the Eastern U.S.A. Its other name tells you exactly how to approach the racket — you 'shake hands' with it.

You can get the feel of this grip by following this simple instruction. Hold your racket straight in front of you with the face vertical to the ground, supporting it with your non-playing hand. Put the palm of your playing hand flat against the face of the racket and slide it all the way down the handle until it reaches the end, the butt. Now wrap your thumb and fingers round the handle, with your forefinger slightly up the handle in a trigger position; this gives you greater control.

Practise this until you can feel the correct grip at once. This grip makes the racket feel like an extension of your hand, so achieving maximum strength and making it easier to play balls of different heights.

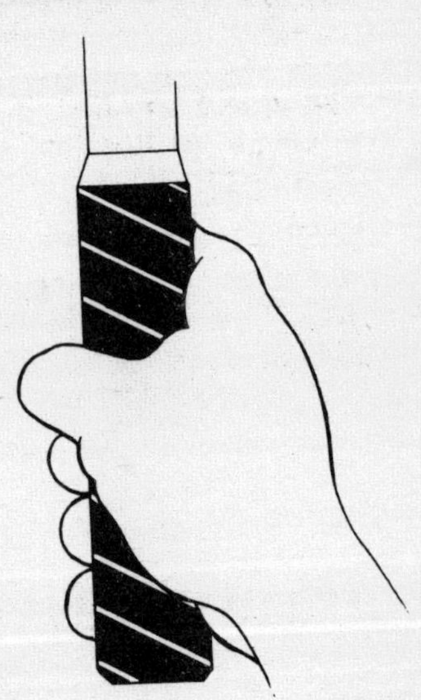

BACKHAND GRIP — drives and volleys

With the backhand you hit the ball with the other surface of the racket strings. The grip has to be adjusted for this and the palm of your playing hand is more on top of the racket with the thumb diagonally across the back.

You get your hand into this grip by turning it inwards a quarter of a turn. To check that you have moved your hand into the right position, put the forefinger of your non-playing hand on the top inner edge of the racket head and run it all the way down the handle.

If your finger comes directly into the 'V' formed between your thumb and first finger on your playing hand, your grip is correct.

You should always support the racket at the throat (where the shaft and the face join) whenever you change grip.

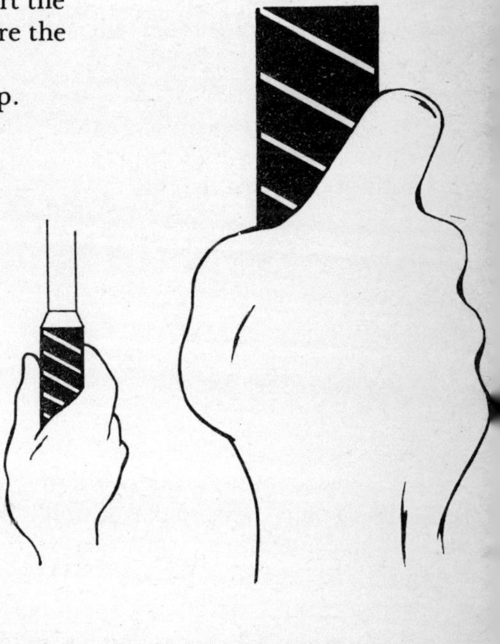

This is a sensitive grip as well as being strong. It gives strength behind the handle but also allows increased flexibility.

TWO-HANDED BACKHAND GRIP

Two-handed backhands are becoming increasingly popular with young players who may not be strong enough to play with a single handed backhand. Using two hands on the backhand side adds strength to control the racket face and the swing, and the extra hand provides increased power for hitting the ball.

The grip you will want to use is formed simply by adding the extra hand to the forehand grip.

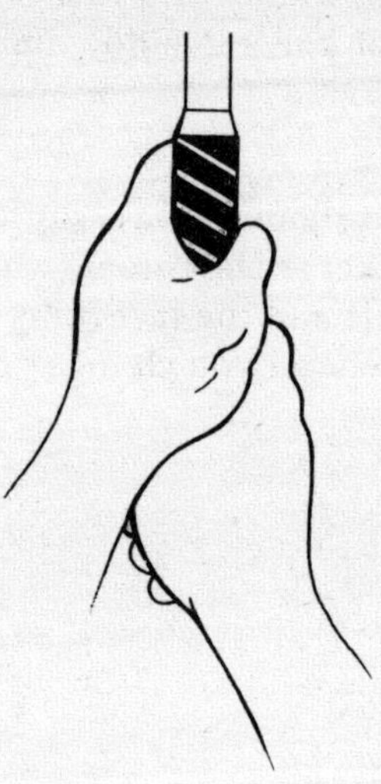

The disadvantage of a two-handed backhand is that it limits your reach. This makes it much more important for a two-handed backhand player to get into a good position to play the stroke; during a fast rally this can be difficult to do. Many players start with a two-handed backhand grip and later change to a one-handed stroke when they are older and stronger. Whichever you use make sure that it is the one best suited to you. **Don't play with a two-handed backhand just because your favourite player does**.

As your game develops you may well want to change your grip if you decide to stay with a two-handed backhand. From the first grip you should advance to the grip in which your right hand is in the backhand grip and your left hand in the **forehand grip**, hands close together. Get a coach to show you.

SERVICE GRIP

Beginners usually start with the forehand grip and change to the '**chopper**' grip as they get more confident. This grip is between the forehand grip and the backhand grip and it gives a better throwing action needed for the service as well as more speed to the ball.

The grip gets its name from the way in which you would hold a small wood chopper or hatchet.

RACKET AND BALL EXERCISES

Trying to hit the ball with racket may feel strange at first, so don't be tempted to clout it as hard as you can. Speed and power can come later, once you have learned how to hit the ball accurately, and this control comes from the throwing exercises that you will have done beforehand. Your racket has to be controlled in different ways for the variety of shots that you will play so it's important to develop the feeling that the racket is part of you, an extension of your hand and arm which meets the ball with the same control and accuracy with which you were catching the ball in one hand.

1. Start by holding the racket in the forehand grip and bounce a ball between the ground and the surface of the strings.

Check that you are holding your wrist firm and that you are raising your arm well above the ball. What you must avoid doing is slapping the ball from the wrist.

2. Using the same grip and the same face of the racket try bouncing a ball in the air. Keep it bouncing, moving your arm as before, for as long as you can.

3. Repeat these exercises using the backhand grip.

4. Now try hitting the ball in the air instead of bouncing it. Hit it gently at first and when you are more confident hit it higher. Then alternate high hits with low hits. Remember to keep your grip and wrist firm as you hit the ball. Feel the difference in power needed for the high hits and the low hits.

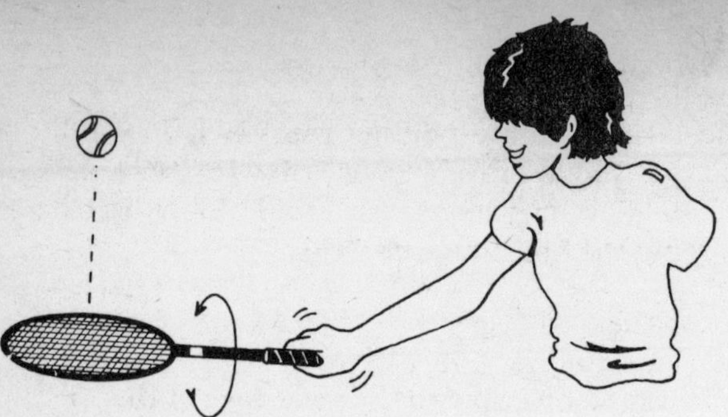

5. With the service grip this time bounce the ball in the air and turn the racket to hit it with the other side of the racket face for your second bounce. Keep hitting the ball and turning the racket like this. It will be difficult at first, but with practice it will become easier and the exercise will help strengthen your wrist, which in turn will give you greater control of the racket face.

6. Using the service grip again try and bounce the ball down to the ground using the edge of the racket head. This will require careful concentration on the ball, because your hitting area will be so much narrower. See how many times you can bounce the ball like this without missing.

7. You can gain experience of judging the flight of high balls by throwing a ball high into the air and then pointing your racket upwards with your arm outstretched in the right position that will let the ball land on the top edge of the racket head. You may miss once or twice at first, but once your eye is in, you'll find the practice very useful for dealing with high tennis shots called **lobs**.

STROKE PREPARATION

Ideally all tennis strokes, except for the service should begin at the same position – **the position of readiness**. This is a position you should try to take up after playing one stroke and before you play the next. From this position you can move quickly in the right direction to play whichever stroke is called for.

The position of readiness is a reference point in your game. It helps you collect your thoughts, concentrate on the ball, sharpen your reflexes and generally helps you gather yourself for the next stroke. Often there will be very little time to do this, but if you get into the habit of adopting this stance, you will be alert and prepared to play any stroke anywhere on the court.

When you get into this position you should be facing your opponent. Your racket should be held in a relaxed forehand grip with your non-playing hand supporting the racket head at the throat.

You should aim to have your feet about shoulder width apart. Your knees should be slightly bent and springy. Your eyes need to be fixed on what is happening on the other side of the net. In this position you should feel like a cat ready to spring into action at just the right moment.

When you receive service you go into the position of readiness at the baseline. When you are at the net you may prefer to crouch slightly lower to get your eyes closer to the flight path of the ball. Wherever you stand you should try to place yourself midway between the likely forehand and backhand strokes. This will help you play whichever stroke is needed when the ball is returned to you.

The **service stance**, which you take up when you are about to serve, is described later.

STROKES — GENERAL POINTS

You will obviously want to use your racket to the best effect in every stroke you play. To do this you need to use one of four basic actions: a **swing**, a **throw**, a **punch** and a **push**. Each of these is described in detail later, but as an indication of what is involved, here are the strokes and actions needed for each one:

For the forehand, backhand and attacking lobs **SWING** the racket head.

For the service and smash **THROW** the racket head.

For the drop-shot and defensive lobs **PUSH** with the racket head.

For the half-volley use a **shortened SWING**.

GROUNDSTROKES

Remember that each stroke should start and finish in the position of readiness. Never watch a stroke without being in this position, even if it is a certain winner. Your opponent may just reach the ball in time and if you are caught off your guard, admiring your last shot, you may not be able to make a return, thereby losing a point.

FOREHAND

To play the forehand you will need to hold the racket in the **forehand grip** (described earlier). The forehand is the most natural stroke to play and it is usually a player's most powerful stroke.

Do you remember how you practised catching the ball just after the top of its bounce? This is the point at which you should aim to hit it on the forehand (and backhand). Hitting the ball in this position will give you a regular approach to every ball.

The most natural level at which to hit a ball is when it is between waist and knee height and by aiming to hit it in this zone you will be hitting it in the most comfortable position, and at the point when it starts to slow down after the bounce.

As your experience grows, you will get better at judging the point at which the ball will start to fall. In turn, you will learn when and where to move to position yourself correctly for the forehand stroke (and the backhand when it applies).

A forehand stroke starts in the position of readiness. The moment you know that the ball is coming on your forehand side start turning to your right (if you are right-handed).

Take back the racket, keeping the head up, letting go of the throat with your non-playing hand.

When the racket is well behind you, your weight will be on your right foot, the back foot, and you will be sideways-on to the net

Start the forward swing by making a shallow loop with the racket head from the end of the take-back. Step towards the net with your left foot and your knees slightly bent. Swing the head of the racket to meet the ball in the centre of the strings, just after the top of its bounce and opposite your left hip.

Hit right through the ball, keeping it in contact with the strings for as long as possible and follow through with the swing in the direction of your shot, finishing about head high with your playing arm outstretched.

As you swing through, your weight will move to your left leg allowing your right leg to come through. Your body will turn and you will face the net to go into the position of readiness for the next stroke.

Throughout the stroke your eyes must be fixed on the ball, watching it right onto the strings.

Essentially the forehand is a flowing, looping stroke with a forward swing that rises slightly through the point where the ball is hit. It is important to keep a firm grip on the racket throughout the stroke, particularly at the moment when you hit the ball.

FOREHAND PRACTICE

You can learn a lot about the forehand by practising on your own hitting a ball against a wall. You can use a special portable wall designed for tennis, though a brick wall or a garage door will do just as well. (Mind the paintwork and the windows if you use either of these, however.) Start in the position of readiness. Turn to your forehand side, taking your racket back as you do. Drop the ball in the front and to the side. Now make your shallow loop and start to swing towards the ball as you step towards the wall. Your hit should feel as if you are lifting the ball towards the wall. Follow through and get back into the position of readiness for the rebound.

You may be tempted to hit the ball as hard as you can. Don't. Even a fairly gentle stroke will come off the wall quite quickly and you will learn nothing if you hit the ball so hard that have no chance of returning it with another forehand.

The purpose of the practice is to keep a forehand rally going **for as long as possible**. So start by hitting the ball with a controlled, easy swing and try to keep this going, making sure you go into the position of readiness between strokes. Only when you are able to keep a rally like this going should you start to hit the ball with more power.

You can practise on your own on a tennis court too. Drop the balls as you would in the wall practice and lift the ball over the net going through the motions of the stroke and returning to the position of readiness each time. Practise hitting the ball diagonally across the court and also try hitting down the line, that is hitting towards what would be an opponents backhand (assuming his or her playing hand is the same as your own). Obviously you will need a lot of balls to make this type of practise worthwhile.

If there are two of you you can take it turns to play forehand strokes while the other one throws the ball from the other side of the net. The thrower should bounce the ball on the court and the player with the racket should play a forehand stroke, lifting the ball easily over the net every time. The thrower can practise his or her ball sense by catching the ball before throwing it again. Start by making the game easy for each other and only make it more difficult as your stroke-play improves.

If there are three of you, stand the third player on the back-line behind the thrower and see if the player with the racket can hit the ball so that he or she can catch it. Once you feel confident about your forehand try a rally with a friend. Start with an easy rally, hitting the ball up and down the court, counting the number of hits and seeing how many you can make. Again this is **not** a competition, the two of you are working together to go through the motions of the forehand. Make your strokes controlled and not too powerful and go back to the position of readiness each time.

You'll probably find it easier to start playing near the service line, gradually moving back to the baseline as you get used to the game.

BACKHAND

Many tennis players accept the fact that their backhand is their weakest stroke and make little attempt to improve it. This is a serious mistake because your game can only be as good as your weakest stroke and once an opponent has spotted a weakness in your backhand, he or she will naturally try to force you to play backhand shots in the hope that you will make mistakes.

The backhand certainly feels less natural than the forehand, but there is no reason why it shouldn't be an attacking stroke as well as a purely defensive one. If you can learn to play the backhand correctly from the start, you stand a much better chance of developing a steady stroke to which you can add winning power at the right moments.

The backhand starts in the position of readiness. You will be holding your racket in the forehand position, so the first thing to do when you know the ball is coming to your backhand is to change to the backhand grip.

Start turning to your left (if you are right-handed); this is your backhand side. As you turn, guide your racket back with your non-playing hand.

Bend your elbow and take your playing hand well back. At the end of your take-back your arm should be almost touching your body and your weight should be on your left (back) foot.

You need to turn more playing a backhand stroke than you do with the forehand. In fact you should turns sideways-on to the net with the back of your right shoulder showing to your opponent, while you look over it, watching the ball on to your racket.

Let go of the racket with your non-playing hand; step towards the net with your right foot, shifting your weight on to it as you swing the racket head forwards to meet the ball.

All the forehand practices and exercises mentioned earlier can be applied just as well to the backhand. Start gently at first, concentrating on developing a smooth, flowing stroke, rather than hitting the ball wildly. It's probably best to begin by going through the motions without using a ball. This is known as **shadowing**. Without the need to hit the ball, you can concentrate on moving through the stroke and playing through an imaginary ball just in front of your body and at the correct height. When you can move from the position of readiness comfortably into and through the backhand, that is the time to start hitting a ball thrown by a friend.

The action of turning your playing shoulder to hit the ball will move you from your sideways-on position towards one where you are facing the net. When you have completed your follow through get back into the position of readiness for the return.

BACKHAND PRACTICE

You should aim to hit it in the centre of the racket face, just after the top of its bounce and in front of your right hip. Hit right through the ball and let the racket head follow through in the direction of your shot, moving forwards and up, ending at head height with the elbow straight.

If you can develop the idea of using your weight to hit the ball and your strength to control the racket, you will play a powerful backhand accurately. Using your weight is principally a matter of stepping into the stroke with your body moving with it as you swing. One further point to practise is the change of grip.

At first you will have to look at this to check that your backhand grip is correct. As you change try and feel the difference though, because when you are playing your eyes must be on the ball the whole time and you won't be able to look down at the handle to check that your grip is right. When you are shadowing, learn to 'feel' the grip.

Once you progress from throwing balls for your friend to hitting backhand back over the net, you can use your own racket to play short backhand rallies. Don't be too ambitious at first.

Set yourselves a target of five strokes and see if you can hit five clean backhands in a rally; hitting from one corner to the other. Remember to return to the position of readiness after each stroke and don't scramble through the backhand motions just to hit the ball. This is part of the practice.

At this stage the power in the stroke is less important than the way in which you play it. So, don't try and hit winners every time when you should concentrate on hitting smooth, long, flowing shots.

DOUBLE-HANDED BACKHAND

The double-handed backhand is played in very much the same way as the one-handed stroke. The preparation is slightly different in that most players who use this stroke stand in the position of readiness with their extra hand holding the racket down the shaft rather than at the throat. This helps them quickly adopt the grip for the double-handed backhand.

The movement into the stroke is the same as that for the one-handed backhand. Take the racket back past your left hip (if you are right-handed) at about hitting height. The racket head may point slightly down as you form a shallow loop.

It is necessary to get closer to the ball than with the one-handed backhand because of the restricted reach. There is also more body rotation combined with a form swing from the shoulders. Just as with the one-handed backhand, you should move your weight into the stroke. Hit the ball just in front of your leading hip and follow through in the direction of your stroke to finish at head height.

At a later stage in your game you will find the double-handed backhand very useful for playing topspin backhand strokes.

The practices for this stroke are the same as those mentioned for the one-handed backhand.

GROUNDSTROKES — GENERAL POINTS

Right from the start you want to develop the habit of hitting the ball at the right height above the net. It may be tempting to try and skim the net every time. This looks dramatic and, for the top players, often wins points. But if you study their game carefully you will see that most of their groundstrokes are hit well above the net, with only a few, occasional net skimmers.

There are two reasons for hitting the ball well above the net.

> Firstly, if you allow yourself good clearance when you strike the ball, there will be a margin for any errors you make. In other words if you don't hit the ball quite as you meant to, with a good margin of clearance, it will still clear the net — and in tennis the principal concern must always be to avoid hitting the ball into the net.

> Secondly, if you hit your groundstrokes well up, they will fall at the right length in the other half of the court. Hitting the ball low will cause it to fall short. So, when you are hitting the ball from your baseline to the baseline on the other side of the net, you should aim to strike the ball so that it clears the net by about one metre. Get used to hitting the ball like this and you will find that you will be able to vary your length just by hitting the ball a little lower.

In both forehand and backhand strokes it is important not to let your racket head drop. If you have to play a low ball, get down to it by bending your knees and lower your waist to the ball. In this way your stroke will be unaffected. With both strokes also, try and develop the feeling that the racket head is swinging away from your body to hit the ball.

Once you have practised both groundstrokes on their own, you will want to put them together. At first you may find it simpler to let one player concentrate on his or her forehand, while the other player hits backhand strokes. This will result in you both hitting the ball down the line from forehand to backhand and from backhand back to forehand.

Take it in turns to play first one stroke and then the other. Keep your eyes on the ball. Get into the position of readiness, even though you know the ball will be coming to your prearranged side.

If you are playing the backhand strokes, 'feel' the change in grip. And above all go steadily through the stroke. Your partner can help here by making his or her return controlled, long, easy and not too powerful. You do the same in your return.

These exercises will form an important part of every warm-up you play before a match, so don't dismiss them as something to be forgotten as you improve. They will help you get into the habit of hitting the ball at a good length. When you are moving well and hitting the ball well, you can start to work the two groundstrokes together. Keep playing down the line and then hit, say, one shot in three cross-court, having warned your partner, so that he or she is not caught unawares. Play three more strokes down the line and then let him or her hit a ball cross-court.

If you can keep a steady rally going like this, the time has come to alternate every shot. One of you begins by hitting the ball down the line with a forehand. The other player receives this on the backhand and plays it cross-court. This is received by the first player on the backhand and is hit down the line to the second player's forehand. The second player then hits it cross-court once more, to the first player's forehand and the sequence begins again. This exercise will get you used to moving along the baseline from one corner to the other playing first a forehand and then a backhand, or vice versa. It will also show you the need for watching the ball to judge where it will bounce and where you should play it. Take it in turns hitting down the line and hitting cross-court.

If you can keep a rally going like this, you will be making good progress.

SERVICE

There is only one stroke in tennis that guarantees you the chance of placing the ball exactly where you want it to be – the service. As you've probably seen from watching first-class tennis, a good, attacking service can often win a point outright. A service that does this is called an **ace**. Even if a service doesn't beat an opponent first time, it can still throw him or her off balance and make them play a poor return. All in all you should aim to make your service your most powerful and attacking stroke.

Unfortunately there are many players who are satisfied with just getting the ball over the net and into the service court. This allows them to play tennis, but they never develop beyond a a mediocre level because they lack the attack which can help them serve aces and unsettle the better players found at higher levels of the game.

> The other great advantage of the service is that it is the one stroke which you can play **in your own time**. No opponent can make you hurry your service, as he or she can with any stroke in a rally, and if you watch the leading players, you will see that they all take time to gather themselves and get fully settled before they deliver the actual service. A rushed service is usually a wasted service.

From the introduction to the stroke you may remember that the service requires a **throwing** action. Serving and throwing a ball overarm follow the same lines. In simple terms, the service can be outlined as: placing the ball in the air with one hand, throwing the racket head at it with the other, with both hands working together. No matter what other details are given, that is the basic action. Try and remember that principle and you won't go far wrong.

Since throwing a ball and serving are largely the same, it's a good idea to get the feel for the service by starting with throwing a ball overarm. You can practise this on your own, though practising with a partner is always more enjoyable.

Get as many old balls as you can find, ideally a dozen. Go on to the tennis court and stand behind the baseline at one end. Although you haven't got your racket at this stage, it's a good idea to get used to the service stand, the position in which you should start every service.

Position yourself about 60cm from the centre mark, behind the baseline. You should stand almost sideways-on to the net, but not quite fully sideways-on.

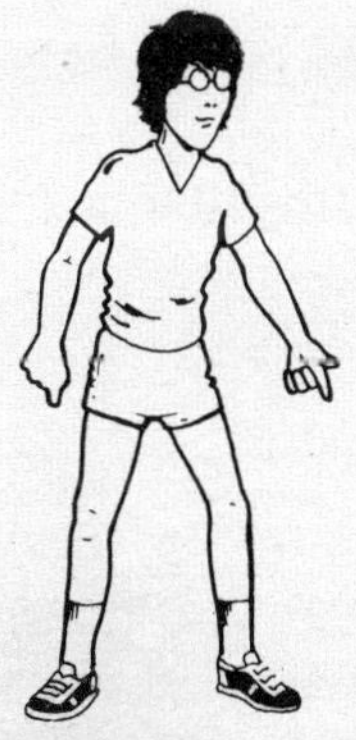

Your front foot should be about a ball's width behind the baseline. Your feet should be as far apart as they are in the position of readiness, (shoulder width) and your knees ought to be flexed slightly.

From the service stance, throw each of the balls into the service court diagonally opposite on the other side of the net. The action you want to aim for is a high overarm throw, with the arm stretched well above your shoulder when you throw. Try for a good, strong throw, increasing your power as the action becomes easier. Use your legs in the throw too by straightening them at the same time as you straighten your arms, giving extra thrust to your action. If there are two of you, you can take it in turns throwing the balls to each other. Throwing exercises like this will help you develop a feel for the service action.

The two key elements of the service are the **placing of the ball in the air** and the **throwing action of the racket head**. Notice that the first part is called 'placing' and not 'tossing' or 'throwing'. Placing suggests care and control and these are essential if you are to have the ball in just the right position when you hit it with your throwing action. You need to be able to place the ball a few centimetres above the top of your fully extended racket, and about 30cm in front of you — and you need to be able to do this time and again for every service, with the same degree of precision. So, let's start with this.

For the time being use just one ball at a time. When you are more experienced you can start serving with two tennis balls in your non-playing hand, but for the moment your hand may be too small, and it's only one more thing to worry about. If you use a double-handed backhand, you'll want to put your other ball in your pocket anyway.

To place the ball in the air for the service, you need to hold it firmly, but lightly, between your thumb and all four fingers.

It is important to make the placing as steady as you can, with no spin on the ball. So keep your hand beneath it all the time and push your arm up until it is fully stretched before releasing the ball. After letting go of the ball bring your arm down carefully. Don't snatch it away.

To practise this use your racket and go through the motions of the service until the point when you should hit the ball, let the ball fall to the ground, however, and see if it lands on a pre-placed target. If it does consistently, you know that your placing is starting to work regularly and effectively.

A racket head cover makes a good target for this practice. You should place it about 30cm it front of you and directly beneath where your place up should go.

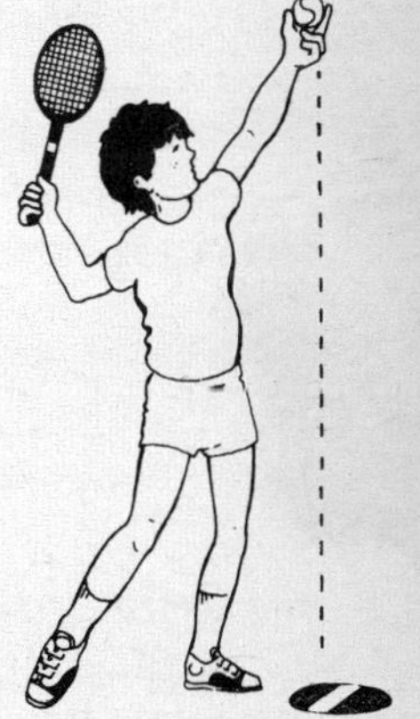

Although the service can be broken down into stages for reasons of description, it's important to get used to going through the motions in a continuous movement. If you get into the habit of doing one part of the service and then another, you will never have the fluid, easy action from which comes power and real attacking drive. So practise your placing by landing the ball on a target, but remember that this is just an aid. Once you can do it, put the exercise to one side and concentrate on hitting the ball in one, smooth, controlled action.

Bearing that in mind, these are the elements that make up the service.

You begin in the **service stance**, using the forehand grip as a beginner, but moving to the chopper grip as soon as you can. Hold the racket in front of you, pointing in the direction in which you want to serve, with the face of the racket vertical to the ground. Hold the ball in your non-playing hand and place it against the strings in the middle of the face. This completes the service stance.

From this position start the service by moving both hands down and away from each other. The playing hand swings the racket back past your legs while the placing hand moves up to place the ball. As your arms part, push your weight forward on to your front foot which will give you a firm base for service.

Let go of the ball when your placing arm is fully stretched, the ball should float directly up as if it is propelled by a fountain of water. At this stage your racket finishes its take-back and you bend your playing arm elbow to bring the racket head across your shoulders.

Without stopping let the racket head drop lower as the ball begins to drop and then start the hitting action by using your wrist to whip up the racket head before bringing your arm up and through the throw, extending it fully so that the racket head hits the ball in the middle of the strings. Your weight should be well over your front foot when you hit the ball and as you follow through let your back foot come forward.

Keep the racket swinging in the direction of your service, finishing as it swings past the other side of your body. At the end of your follow through, your back foot should have come forward and should be firmly planted on the ground to balance you. From this position move into the position of readiness for the return from your opponent.

You must watch that your left (front) foot is secure from the beginning to the end of the stroke. If it is not, you may incur a **foot fault**, as described later.

You will see players serving with several variations of service, using spin and slicing the ball, but these are features that you can add to your game later, once you have mastered this basic service. For the time being concentrate on getting a smooth, balanced action to which you can add increasing power as you improve. Remember that the most accurate service in the world is worth little if it lacks attack. You want to aim at producing the strongest service you can.

A server is allowed two services. If the first service is a fault there is a second chance to serve the ball into the correct service court. If this second service is also a fault, the server has served a double fault and loses the point. If the ball touches the net during a service this is known as a **let** and the server is allowed to serve that service again.

The purpose in mentioning these rules is to show how important concentration is when you are serving. Although you may serve a fault or a let on your first service, it is important not to let this upset you for your second service. Inevitably most people serve a hard first service and a gentler second service in the hope that the second one will land in the service court.

There is the risk that the second service will just become a way of getting the ball in play. Try to avoid this. Although you may want to sacrifice some of your attack to make sure of getting the ball in the service court, you can apply spin to the service which will make it far from easy to return, even though it may not be as fast as your first service. This is a skill you will acquire when you become more experienced. But at this stage avoid falling into the habit of serving a feeble second service.

SERVICE PRACTICE

For the most important stroke in your game it is surprising how little most players practise their service. Obviously you will want to practise serving as a beginner, but service practice should form an important part of your non-match playing no matter at what level of competition you play. Once you have got used to the service action and can apply power without losing control, you will need to turn your attention to accuracy.

The service box may not seem very big from your side of the net, but there are three definite target areas in the box, all of which are used to attack your opponent in different ways.

Most players have a weakness somewhere in their game, as I've mentioned earlier this is often their backhand, certainly at lower levels of the game, so it's natural that you will want to serve against the weakness to unsettle an opponent and force him or her to make a mistake. You can serve to an opponent's forehand, to a backhand, or directly at the opponent's body, which forces him or her to hurry a stroke and usually play it too close to the body. To serve at these targets you need to land the ball on either side of the service court, or in the centre, and this is where accuracy comes in.

The easiest way to practise is to take a large number of balls onto a court and set three targets (racket head covers, ball boxes, plastic cups) in the service court in the two corners, just inside from the service line and midway between these two. Then serve at each of these, serving two balls before moving to the next target. See how many times you can hit the targets and keep a score to better in your next practice.

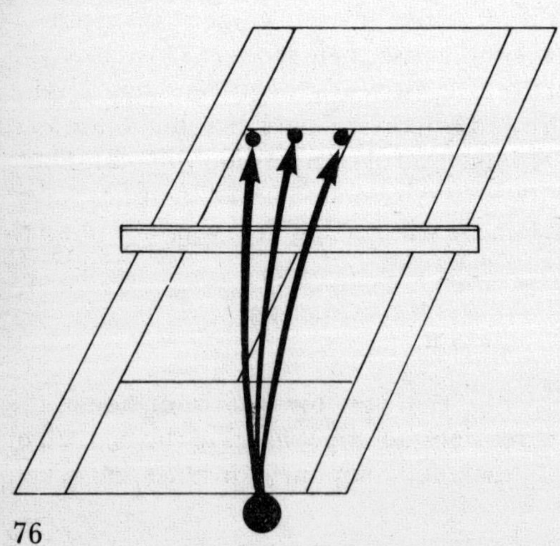

(If you set three more targets in the service court immediately opposite you can practise serving from the other side when you change ends to pick up the balls).

Since the service is so important, here are the principal points once more — a check list for you to run through in your exercises:

1. Get into the service stance, sideways-on to your target and balanced.

2. Put the ball and racket together with both arms pointing towards the service court. Starting together will help your timing.

3. Aim carefully at your target.

4. Move both hands at the same time — one placing the ball up in front of you, the other swinging back the racket.

5. Throw the racket forward and up to hit the ball at highest point you can comfortably reach.

6. Follow through along the line of your aim, then down and across your body.

7. Move immediately into the position of readiness for the return and your next stroke.

8. If your first service is a fault or a let, carefully go through the preparations again, with a fresh balance and a fresh aim.

9. As soon as your service is controlled, add power.

VOLLEYS

The volley, whether forehand or backhand, is the least complicated and the most enjoyable stroke to play. Volleys are played with a short, crisp, simple action before the ball has a chance to bounce (ideally they should be hit before the ball reaches the top of its first flight). They are usually played at the net as a means of catching an opponent off guard. Volleys require quick reactions, but they offer a good chance of hitting winners, too.

As volleys are played on both the forehand and the backhand it's understandable to think of them as shortened versions of the groundstrokes. The action and feel of playing a volley is quite different, however; instead of swinging the racket head at the ball, it is **punched** at the ball.

> The grip for a forehand volley is the same as that for a forehand groundstroke, likewise the backhand volley has the same grip as the backhand groundstroke.

FOREHAND VOLLEY

The position for readiness at the net, where most volleys are played, is much the same as that on the baseline, except that most players prefer to bend their knees a little more.

The moment you see the ball coming to your forehand, lift the racket with a short take-back in line with the approaching ball.

Because the stroke is a punch and not a swing, you must avoid taking the racket back too far; it should go no further back than your shoulder. Your elbow should be well bent since much of the power in the stroke comes from straightening your arm.

Step forwards with your left foot (if you are right-handed) and move your weight onto that foot as you move to punch the ball. You'll have to keep your wrist very firm as you make contact with the ball to the side and in front of you, hitting through it with the full face of your racket strings.

The follow through is short with the racket head slightly above the level of your wrist and as soon as this is finished you must return to the position of readiness for the next stroke.

BACKHAND VOLLEY

The position of readiness for the backhand volley is the same as the one for the forehand volley. This means that you will have to change to the backhand grip as soon as you see the ball coming to your backhand side, while you lift the racket.

You should take the racket-head back on the same line as the approaching ball, or the height at which you are going to play it. Again you ought not take the racket head further back than your shoulder; doing this encourages you to make too wide a swing.

At the completion of your take-back your non-playing hand should still be holding the racket at the throat.

As you step forward with your right-foot, release the racket throat and punch the racket head forwards to hit the ball to the side but well in front of your body.

Hit through the ball with a short follow through and then turn to face the net to move into the position of readiness once more.

VOLLEYS — GENERAL POINTS

Volleys really fall into two categories. The ones above the height of the net are **attacking volleys**, while the ones below the level of the net are **defensive volleys** which means that you have to bend your knees to get right down to them.

Whenever possible **step in** to play a volley. This makes for power and helps your balance, as well as ensuring a quick recovery.

Volleying directly at your opponent's body will force him or her to make a hurried stroke and could well win you the point. If your opponent volleys directly at your body the easiest way of dealing with the stroke is to play a backhand volley which is less severely affected by being played close to the body.

VOLLEYING PRACTICE

On your own you can't beat volleying against a wall to get the idea of fast reactions, limited take-back and solid punching with a good, firm wrist. At first you'll no doubt prefer to stay in the sideways-on position to punch at the ball, particularly if you stand only two metres from the wall.

Don't let yourself move further back to gain more time between strokes. This will only encourage you to swing the racket head too far back. You may feel rushed playing so close to the wall, but volleys require fast, sharp action. Stick at it and you'll soon enjoy seeing how many vollies you can play in a rally.

Don't stay in this sideways position for too long. Remember the position of readiness and try to get back to that between shots. Aiming at a target on the wall will help improve your accuracy too.

Practising on a court can take the same form as your practices for the groundstrokes, if you have a partner with whom to practise. One of you can stand on the service line and throw the ball to the other player standing near the other side of the net. The player with the racket has to try and volley the ball back to the thrower.

> If you can volley it so accurately that he or she doesn't have to move from the spot where they are standing, then your volleying will be getting pretty accurate.

Go back to the position of readiness between strokes as the ball may come to either your backhand or your forehand. Once you have both had some practice, the thrower should vary the throws from one side to the other, so that the volleyer has to watch the ball carefully to judge which side to receive it.

LOBS

The lob is a high shot, hit like a groundstroke, which sends the ball sailing over your opponent's head forcing him or her to run to back of their court to retrieve it.

As a **defensive shot**, the lob can get you out of difficulties when an opponent has played a smash, which you have managed to reach, by giving you time to settle yourself and get to the centre of the court once more.

As an **attacking shot** it can force an opponent from the net deep into his or her own court, so giving you the opportunity to move forward and volley their return. Sometimes the lob can even be an outright winner.

In hitting a lob you should aim to land it near the baseline, within two metres. You need to hit it up too, just high enough to be out of your opponent's reach.

For safety's sake it's usually wisest to lob to your opponent's backhand side, so forcing him or her to reply with the more difficult backhand smash. The wind and the sun can be helpful in lobbing too. A strong breeze can blow a lobbed ball off its anticipated flight. Provided you know how to adjust your stroke to allow for the wind, the stroke can work to your advantage and against your opponent. Similarly if you are playing with the sun behind you, a lob will force your opponent to look into the sun to smash the ball. This makes the shot all the more difficult.

The forehand and backhand lobs are played with the same preparation as similar groundstrokes. After taking the racket back, however, you should swing the head towards the ball with the bottom edge leading; this will help give the ball lift.

You should aim to hit the ball opposite your leading hip, swinging the head up and through it.

The basic lob is hit almost as if you were hitting the ball with your hand instead of the racket. To give the ball height, therefore, you need to follow through with the racket head rising steeply, following the ball as it sails up and over the net, with the racket head finishing high above the head, pointing along the ball's flight path.

Many people fall into the error of playing their lobs too gently, with the result that they either fall short or never climb high enough to avoid being smashed. **The farther back in the court you play a lob, the bolder your swing must be**.

Remember to try and land your lobs in the rear two metres of your opponent's court. This will make him or her scramble back to retrieve it and may even force an error, which could give you the point.

LOBBING PRACTICE

On your own you can practise lobbing from your baseline into an area of the other court marked by a line two metres in from the baseline. This should be your target area. You might try lobbing over a partner, holding a racket in an outstretched hand, to get a feeling for clearing an opponent standing near the net. Ask your partner to throw the ball to you to ensure accuracy in feeding you the balls. Once you have both learned to smash the ball, you will be able to practise lobbing and smashing together, with one of you performing one stroke and the other practising the other stroke.

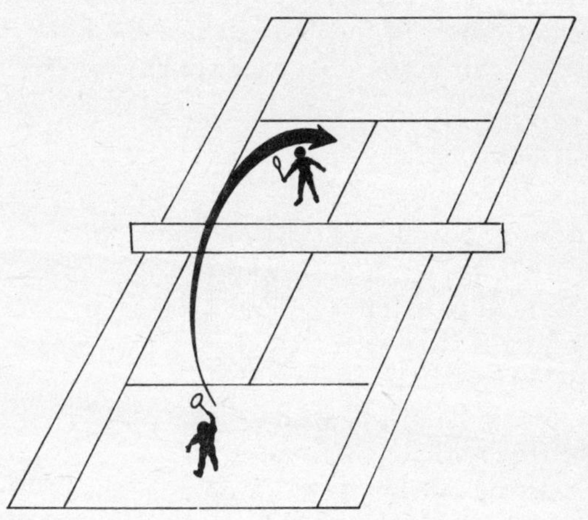

As with all the basic strokes mentioned here, there are variations in the lob involving spin and lobbing on the volley, but these are skills that you can learn later once you are confident in the basic actions. It is a mistake to introduce too many alternatives in the early stages when a beginner might easily confuse two different strokes and fail to play the basic stroke, on which all the others depend.

SMASH

The smash is most players' answer to the lob. It is the stroke used to kill a poor lob and often win a point by hitting it hard and wide, away from an opponent. It's an exciting stroke to play and watch and it has several variations, but the basic smash follows similar lines to the service stroke — they both require the racket head to be thrown at the ball.

Unlike the service, you can't decide where the ball will be when you hit a smash. That depends on where your opponent chooses to hit it. Although positioning for the smash is more difficult than it is for the service, there is less need for you to produce great power in the stroke, since the falling ball will already have a fair amount of pace which you can use.

The position for a smash is underneath the ball, just as it would be if you wanted to catch it in your hands. Timing is vital with a good smash. Hitting the ball too near the top of the racket head will send it into the net; hitting too late will send it over the baseline. So you have watch it carefully right on to the strings.

It is important to prepare yourself early for a smash, so get your racket into the throwing position without going through the swing that you would use in the service (you should use your service grip). Stand as you would for a service, that is almost sideways-on to the net with the racket across the back of your shoulders.

The difficulty in the smash lies in judging the speed of the ball and timing the stroke so that you hit it with your racket arm fully extended (in the service you can place the ball for yourself, in the smash this is impossible, of course). Many players point their non-playing hands in the direction of the ball while they are smashing.

This helps them in their judgement and positioning and it also gives the same feeling in hitting the ball as they get from serving, when the non-playing hand places the ball in the air.

Once you have thrown the racket head at the ball, the follow through is the same as that for the service, with the racket head following in the direction of your stroke and then swinging down past the body before you move into the position of readiness, which you must do, even if you are certain the smash is going to be a winner. (Moving to the position of readiness should become second nature to you).

The art of playing a good smash is in your positioning. If your opponent has sent a lob over your head, you may well have to run backwards while watching the ball and before throwing the racket head at it. This takes great concentration and needs a lot of practice in judging ball-flight and speed. That's why the shortened throwing action is best when you have little time to prepare the stroke.

Unless it is absolutely necessary do not let a ball bounce before smashing it. The sooner you can return a lob, the less time it will give your opponent and if he or she has played a defensive lob to get out of trouble, the quicker you return it with a smash, the less time there will be for their recovery and the more chance you stand of winning the point. If possible, you should always jump for a smash. This isn't easy, of course, and it takes considerable skill and experience to play it effectively. Watching the ball right on to the strings is the key.

To be successful you must treat a smash as a full-blooded, attacking shot. Play each one as a potential winner. There can't be any half-measures with a smash. Either you hit it positively, or you fluff the shot. At the same time you can't afford to lose control. The ball will already have some pace and you must use this as well as your own power to send it on its way. There is always a great temptation to belt a smash for all you're worth, particularly when it looks easy, but guard against this. Hit the ball firmly, but not wildly, and if you're in a bad position to play the stroke, cut down your power too.

Accuracy is important in the smash, as it is in the service. The purpose of the stroke is to win the point, so you'll need to play it in the way that makes it most difficult for your opponent to reach. A smash deep into your opponent's court will usually win the point, but use the short, angled smash as well, to avoid making your play too predictable.

Whenever possible take a smash on your forehand, even if it means you have to run further to run round onto your forehand side. The forehand smash is easier and more powerful than the backhand one and you will stand a much greater chance of success if you use it. The backhand smash is a useful stroke to learn later, but in the early stages stick to perfecting your forehand smash.

Here, in brief, are the main points behind the smash:

1. Use your service grip.
2. Watch the ball.
3. Move to get underneath it while you take your racket back behind your shoulders.
4. Throw the racket head at the ball with your arm coming full stretch.
5. At the end of the stroke your shoulders should have turned from being sideways-on to facing the net.
6. Try to watch the ball right on to the strings.
7. Follow through down and across your body.
8. Move into the position of readiness.

SMASH PRACTICE

By far the best way to practise your smash is on court with a partner who can lob balls to you. This will give you both practice. While one works on the lob, the other can work on the smash.

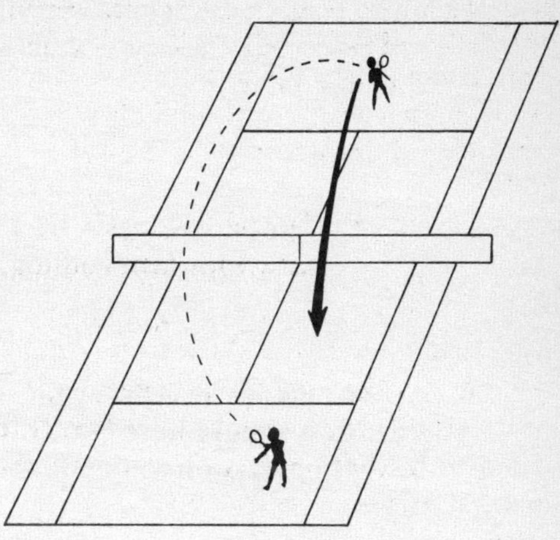

Try, say, a quarter of an hour of one stroke and then swap.

You might like to vary this by adding some drives and volleys. Try following a deep lob, which is smashed, with a short drive that brings you into the net to play a volley. Get your partner to return this with a lob deep into your court and run back to smash this once more. This will get you used to running back under pressure to smash a lob, and then immediately coming forward to play a volley.

DROPSHOT

As its name suggests, the dropshot is not a stroke that depends on great power for its success. The idea is to make the ball drop just over the net and bounce very little, making it impossible for your opponent to play it before the second bounce.

Dropshots are the most delicate shots you will play and they need control and careful angling of the racket head to be successful. The success of the dropshot depends on the skilful use of backspin, which is difficult to apply at first.

The dropshot really comes into the category of advanced strokes, since you can play a game of tennis, and win, without needing to use it. However, the basic actions of the dropshots are similar to those used for playing volleys and if you learn to play a dropshot effectively, it will be a very useful stroke to use once in a while; but remember it is not a stroke you play right at the start of your coaching.

> Essentially the dropshot is a surprise stroke, not one that you use in every rally. Used unexpectedly when your opponent is at the back of his or her court, it can catch them unawares and throw them off their guard. You can win a point with a dropshot and unsettle an opponent, but dropshots alone won't win a match.

Before you start to play a dropshot of any sort it is a good idea to practise the backspin and get a feel of the way to apply it.

Start by dropping a ball from head height and trying to slide your racket, edge first, underneath it, with the aim of hitting it straight up in the air loaded with backspin. Let this ball land and see how it bounces sharply in the opposite direction to that of the racket.

That is the way backspin works — the ball cuts back. Therefore, you can see that if you play a dropshot that lands just over the net and play it with backspin, the ball will cut back towards the net, making it almost impossible for your opponent to reach. You'll find this exercise difficult to begin with so don't worry if it takes you time to judge when to hit the ball.

When you feel confident at doing this, start to move the ball forwards with backspin. This requires the racket to be angled.

Again start gently, by just showing your strings a little more to the net. Now drop the ball and hit it with the racket held at this angle. This time the ball will move a little nearer the net, though still with backspin.

Carry on gradually showing the strings to the net and hitting the ball with backspin until the ball clears the net by about 30cm and drops just over the other side.

Watch how the backspin stops the ball from bouncing sharply towards your opponent. You can add more backspin by slicing the racket down to hit the bottom edge of the ball.

The stroke action for the forehand and the backhand is like that used for playing volleys, except that instead of punching the ball along the line of its flight, you play the dropshot by pushing the racket head down the back of and underneath the ball to give it spin. You should aim to hit the ball just in front of you and to the side, as you would hit a groundstroke, because although the dropshot is played with the same action as a volley it is hit after the ball has bounced.

Dropshots hit before the ball bounces are called **drop volleys**. These are played with the normal volley action but the punching action is replaced by a simple blocking motion. The aim of the drop volley is to take the pace off the ball and this can be improved by slightly drawing the racket head back at the moment of impact to deaden the flight of the ball. You can give the ball backspin by slightly tilting the racket face backwards.

The drop volley is best played very near the net, where it is much easier to play than further back in the court, though with this and all other strokes played at the net you must remember not let your racket stray over the net itself, which is against the rules.

DROPSHOT PRACTICE

For practising on your own you can mark target areas on the other side of the net a couple of metres deep and practise dropshots from your own service court, trying to land the ball between the net and the outer limit of your target area. Practise both forehand and backhand dropshots, developing your control of the backspin on both sides.

Do not try to do a dropshot from the back of the court, it is too difficult. Try it with balls which land on the service line.

A WORD ABOUT SPIN

Topspin, backspin, sidespin, slices, spins of every sort can be applied to all the strokes that have been outlined to help with ball control; they give variety in the speed of the ball and affect its bounce.

In the description of the dropshot there was an exercise for the backspin and by using similar practices you will come to see how topspin and sidespin work. The action for topspin is the opposite of that for backspin, because the aim of the spin is opposite too. Topspin makes the ball spin forwards after it has bounced, so that it appears to leap forward towards your opponent. In a similar way sidespin makes the ball swerve to one side or the other.

To apply **topspin** to a stroke the racket head needs to brush over the top of the ball after coming up from below. This hitting up and over action makes the ball spin forward and helps to keep it up for longer than it would if there was no spin. Balls with top spin approach the court at a steep angle and bounce higher and further than those hit with no spin. You can increase topspin by loosening your wrist and whipping the strings up and over the ball.

For **sidespin** you need to draw the strings across the ball. Adding sidespin to a forehand stroke will require you to start to the right of the ball (if you are right-handed). If you want to add sidespin to a backhand stroke you need to start drawing the racket strings across the ball from the left (again assuming you are right-handed).

In both cases the ball will rotate sideways during its flight, swerving in the opposite direction to its rotation.

By combining topspin or backspin with sidespin, you can make the ball perform a mixture of swerves and leaps that will confuse and unsettle your opponent. However, it is important to understand how spins can affect your strokes.

Don't use spin just for the sake of using it; have a definite purpose in mind, as in the dropshot, where it kills the ball and stops it bouncing too much.

There are many more advanced strokes which you can learn that incorporate spins and slices with the basic strokes that have been outlined here. These are strokes that you should learn from a professional coach once you have a good understanding of the basic strokes and once your technique is sound enough to start introducing a few modifications.

POSITIONS

SINGLES

After the toss and when the decision has been taken as to which player will stand at which end and who will serve first, the server and his opponent take up their positions for the start of the first game.

The server should usually stand just to the side of the centre mark, behind the baseline, as described in the section on serving. It is important to make sure that your feet remain behind the baseline until you have actually struck the ball. If one of your feet touches or crosses the line this is a **foot fault** and you will have lost your first service through a needless error. This position near the centre of the baseline allows the server to move to either a forehand or a backhand return with almost equal ease.

The receiver, usually stands a metre behind the baseline between the inner tramline and the centre mark.

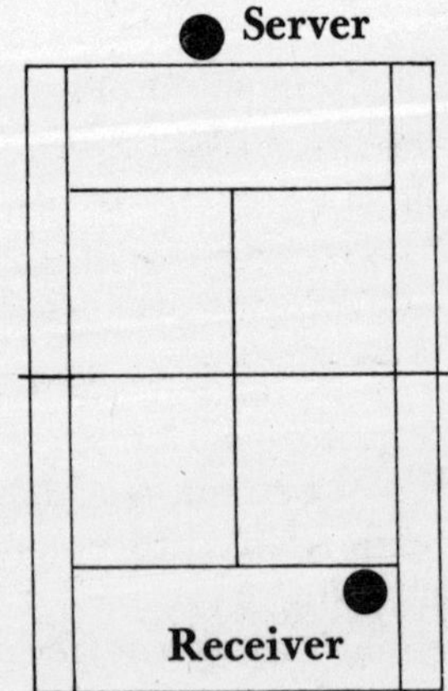

Neither of these position is fixed, however. A server aiming for an angled serve to the side of his opponent's court may move further from the centre, and in the course of the game he or she will want to change the angle of the service to stop the receiver anticipating where it will bounce. Likewise the receiver may well wish to stand further back or further forward depending on the speed of the service and different types of service are returned more easily from some positions than others. Choose a position which will give you the greatest advantage at the service.

Once the ball is in play, there are two principal positions in the court from where a player can most easily cover his or her court.

For playing groundstrokes a position about a metre behind the centre of the baseline will give a good command of the court, while a volleyer will want to stand astride the centre line about 2.5m from the net.

If you can get to one of these two positions after every shot and be waiting in the position of readiness for the return, you will be very well placed to control the play, but in the heat of a match this will not always be possible. It's something to aim for anyhow.

DOUBLES

With two players to cover a doubles court, the server can afford to stand midway between the centre-mark and the outside tramline; in this position he and his partner will be well placed to cover the whole court. The server's partner should stand 2.5m from the net and just over a metre inside the inner tramline, from here he or she will be able to move into volley at the net, while also being able to run back and smash any lobs played by the opposing players.

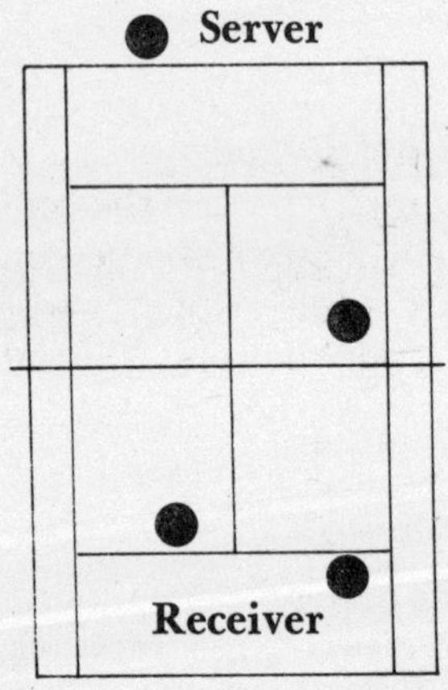

The receiver should stand in the same place as the receiver in a singles game while his or her partner should stand near the service line about 2m to the side of the centre line. This is the best position from which to watch the server's partner and from which to move to intercept any returns.

TACTICS FOR SINGLES

1. Find out your opponent's weakness and play on it.

2. Try to make your opponent play long returns which will limit the angles at which he or she can make shots.

3. Always try to come in to the net on a good, deep, shot, moving in on the side of the court where you have played the shot.

4. The best way of dealing with players who like playing shots on the run is to aim your returns to bounce at their feet. These are very difficult to deal with if you are on the move.

5. At a more advanced stage, if you play a good dropshot, go the net. From here you will be able to volley your opponent's return or even play a second dropshot if the occasion demands.

TACTICS FOR DOUBLES

1. Play as a team. Two players who play well together, who help and encourage each other, will often beat two who are better individually but who play doubles as individuals with no teamwork.

2. Try to cover any weaknesses in your partner's game and he or she will do the same for you.

3. If your partner serves a fault, don't look round. You may only mean to give encouragement, but your face will distract the server and might lead to a double fault.

4. Cover the gaps made when your partner is forced wide.

5. Try to get to the net faster than your opponents and get there together.

6. Use angled shots rather than deep ones since angled shots open up gaps in your opponents' defence and give you the chance to hit into them.

7. Hitting down the middle of the court has its advantages at times. It limits the range of shots open to your opponents by removing many of the angles and there is the chance that both of them will go for the ball, causing confusion and making them miss the ball completely.

8. Direct your play at the weaker of the two opponents and also on their individual weaknesses.

MATCH OFFICIALS — WHO THEY ARE AND WHAT THEY DO

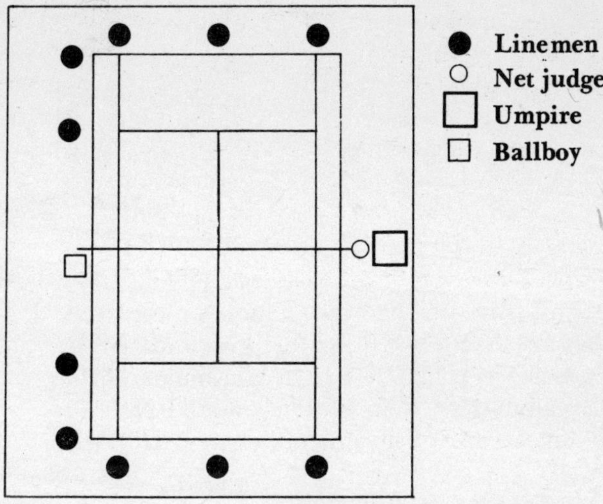

There is sometimes confusion among members of the public over what is the role of the umpire as opposed to the referee. The problem probably arises because these two titles are used in different sports to describe the people who do largely the same job. An umpire in cricket supervises the game and makes sure that the players play according to the rules and in football or rugby the same job is done by the refereee. In tennis the referee and the umpire have two distinct jobs.

> The **referee** is the person who is in overall charge of a tournament and who makes all the decisions.

In recent years the referee has been more in evidence at Wimbledon, for example, where players have challenged decisions made by other officials. In cases like this, the referee has the final say.

The **umpire**, on the other hand, is the person who calls and keeps the score during a match. If you have seen matches played in major world tournaments like Wimbledon you will have seen the umpire sitting up in a tall chair next to the net.

The umpire has an overall view of the court and he or she has the controlling decision in a match, however there are other officials to assist in controlling the game; these are the **line judges**.

In championships and tournaments, the **linesmen** are qualified umpires themselves. They are spread around the court, well back from the playing area and seated in positions that allow them an uninterrupted view of the lines they are judging. Each linesman is responsible for calling faults and deciding points on his or her line alone. If any linesman is unsighted the umpire has the final say.

During the gaps between rallies, **ball-boys** and **girls** field loose balls on the court and give them to the server when requested.

DEVELOPING YOUR GAME

Tennis is not an easy game to learn and at times may seem a very long way from hitting a tennis ball in the garden at home to playing at Wimbledon, but, if it's any comfort, all of the players you watch in the great world championships had to start just as you are starting. They had to work their way through higher and higher levels of tennis until they emerged at the top. Improving and developing your game is not something that will happen without a great deal of effort and a lot of time, but it isn't something that you can't plan either. There are recognized levels of tennis through which you can pass, measuring your improvement as you go, gaining experience and confidence.

There are five principal aims you should have in the back of your mind – five standards you should aim to reach. They are:

1. To play a game.
2. To play for your school and/or club junior team.
3. To get selected for County coaching.
4. To get selected for Regional Training.
5. To get selected for National Training.

Competition is the way to make the greatest overall advances. Try to get as much competition as you can. Play with players slightly better than yourself; enter school tournaments and competitions; enter club tournaments and competitions; and enter the L.T.A. junior tournaments.

Coaching from a Professional Coach will give you a sound technique. You can obtain a list of recognized, fully qualified coaches from the secretary of the **Professional Tennis Coaches' Association**: –

Mrs. P.M.
Bocquet,
21 Glencairn Court,
Lansdown Road,
Cheltenham,
Gloucestershire,
GL50 2NB

(Enclose a stamped, addressed envelope)

There are various grades of coaches according to the level of qualification each has reached. The highest level of coaching qualification is the **L.T.A. Registered Professional Coach**, which requires passing Part III of the L.T.A. Training of Coaches examination. Next comes the **L.T.A. Assistant Coach**, which shows that the holder has passed Part II of the L.T.A. Training of Coaches examination. Then there is the **L.T.A. Elementary Tennis Teacher**. Holders of this qualification have passed the Elementary Teachers Certificate examination.

If you are thinking of taking tennis coaching it is far better to go to a qualified coach. They are trained to teach players of all standards and will know the problems faced by young players and how they can most easily be overcome.

Near the beginning, I mentioned the simple test for near beginners which you might enjoy setting as one of your first tennis achievements. This is the **The Lawn Tennis Performance Award**, which is aimed at setting a standard of performance. If you pass the examination you will receive a badge and certificate. This is what the examination involves.

There are two standards of award – **yellow** (Elementary) and **white** (Advanced). The yellow award is designed for players aged 9 to 12 and the white award is more within the reach of school team players. The examination is much the same for both awards, but a higher standard is demanded from the white award candidates who are expected to show an understanding of spin as well as the ability to play volleys and smashes in a game.

The examination lasts between 15 and 20 minutes and falls into four sections, all of which have to be passed to gain the award:

Section 1

Basic strokes: forehand drives, backhand drives, services, forehand volleys, backhand volleys and alternate volleys played from balls fed by the examiner.

Section 2

4 rallies with the examiner varying the pace and length. A rally of 10 strokes is needed for the Elementary Award and one of 20 strokes is required for the Advanced Award. You have 4 possible attempts at each and for the Advanced Award you must play at least 4 or 5 backhand drives.

Section 3

2 games with the examiner serving for one game and the candidate serving for the other. The candidate has to keep score and Advanced award candidates have to use both the volley and the smash.

Section 4

Assessment, based on the two games. In this section the candidate is examined on his or her ability to play a game, to assess the opponent's strokes and to respond to his or her returns correctly. Advance award candidates are expected to show an understanding of the way that spin can affect a ball.

The examiners are all qualified Professional Tennis Coaches and you have to pay a small fee for taking the exam. The examiner will tell you whether you have passed or failed as soon as the exam is over. If you have passed the result will be sent to the secretary of the P.T.C.A. and you will receive a certificate showing your grade and a badge which you can sew on to your tennis kit.

For full details of the scheme and an outline of the exam write to the organiser, Mrs. P.M. Bocquet in Cheltenham, whose address was given earlier.

FAMOUS PLAYERS

Sue Barker

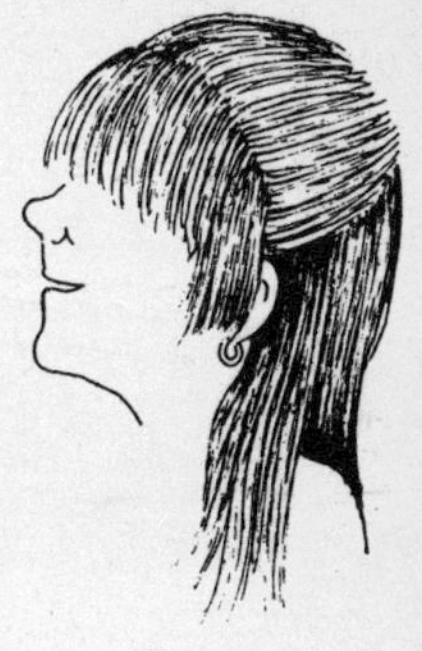

Sue Barker was born in Devon where she was coached by the well-known West Country coach, Arthur Roberts, who had also coached other leading British players, among them Mike Sangster and Angela Mortimer. When she was 15 Sue won the Green Shield British junior title on both wood and grass.

Three years later, in 1975, she played in the first British team to win the Wightman Cup since 1925. But her golden year was 1976. In the final of the French women's championship she beat Renata Tomatova, whom she also beat later in the year to capture the German title also. So great was her success that year that she was voted the most improved player of the year by the Women's Tennis Association. (In winning the French title she became the first British player to take the crown for ten years; the last British success having been with Ann Haydon Jones in 1966). In 1977 Sue was runner-up to Chris Evert (as she then was) in the Virgina Slims championship finals, and also runner-up to Evonne Cawley in the New South Wales Open. Things didn't go all Sue's way in the years that followed, but with her customary determination she persevered, overcame her difficulties and returned to the top of the ladder of British women's tennis at the start of the 1980's.

Bjorn Borg

If you want an image for the new style of tennis that swept across the world's championships from the mid-1970's, you need only look at Bjorn Borg. In 1972, when he was aged 15, Bjorn Borg won the Wimbledon junior invitation event and played for Sweden in the Davis Cup.

In 1973 he was seeded No. 6 at Wimbledon and was mobbed by thousands of teenage fans who flocked to see the handsome, blonde Swede. Cool as ever, Borg didn't let this affect his play and, young as he was, he reached the quarter finals. When he was just 18 he won the US professional title and retained it for the following two years, 1975 and 1976. From then on Borg seemed unbeatable. His famous double-handed backhand, his vicious use of spin, his remarkable athleticism and primarily his total concentration marked him out as the leading player of the decade.

In 1976 he became the third youngest player to win the Wimbledon men's singles and he won that title for the next four year as well, so setting the longest sequence of wins in the history of the championship. He won the French championship in 1974, 1975, and from 1978–81. He was WCT (World Championship Tennis) champion in 1976, winner of the Grand Prix Masters Tournament in 1979 and 1980 and was designated world champion by the International Tennis Federation from 1978–80. After his long run of successes the champion finally seemed to meet his match in 1981 when he found himself runner-up to John McEnroe at Wimbledon. Borg played only a few tournaments in 1982 and retired early in 1983. In future he will play exhibition matches.

Lew Hoad

One of the greatest Australian players and ranked as one of the greatest players of all time, Lew Hoad was a leading figure in world tennis in the 1950's. With Ken Rosewall, a rival from his school days, Hoad dominated world tennis. When they were both only 19 they were responsible for winning the Davis Cup for Australia in 1953.

Hoad's singles match against the American, Tony Trabert, is rated by many as being the greatest Davis Cup match ever played. The first set alone took 90 minutes and with the score at 5–5 in the final set and Hoad 0–30 down, he fought back, in pouring rain, and won 7–5. In 1956 and 1957, Lew Hoad became the first player since the Second World War to win Wimbledon two years running. He would have made the grand slam in 1956 too had Rosewall not beaten him to take the US championship. After winning at Wimbledon for the second time Hoad turned professional, though from then on he suffered from back trouble. In 1968 and 1970, however, he returned to play at Wimbledon.

Jimmy Connors

Jimmy Connors was 19 when he reached the Wimbledon quarter-finals in 1972, a year in which he won $90,000 in prize money. Connors symbolizes the hard-hitting style of play that has come to be known as power tennis. He fights every point, hits every shot as a winner and races to the net to volley his opponent's return with savage power and accuracy.

Although Connors has only won the Wimbledon title twice, in 1974 and 1982, he has always been a major force for his opponents to overcome. While in America he was the leading player until the arrival of the even more aggressive John McEnroe. In 1973 he won the the Wimbledon men's doubles with Ilie Nastase, at his first attempt (Two years later they won the US. title). He won the US Open in 1974, 1978 and 1982. He won the Australian singles title in 1974 also. In 1977 he was WCT champion in the same year he won the Grand Prix Masters tournament and in 1978 he was Grand Prix Winner with a higher total of points in major tournaments than any other player. In 1980 he again won the WCT singles tournament.

Jimmy Connors also holds the record for winning the highest prize money offered in a single game, half a million dollars which he won when he beat John Newcombe in a challenge match in 1975.

Billie Jean King

Like Bjorn Borg in the 1970's, Billie Jean King dominated Wimbledon in the 1960's. She made her first visit when she was 17 and won her first event, the women's double's, with Karen Hantze that year. In 1963 she reached her first Wimbledon singles finals, where she was beaten by Margaret Smith. In 1966 she won the Wimbledon championship for the first time.

The following year she won the singles, the women's doubles (with Rosemary Casals) and the mixed doubles with Owen Davidson. In 1967 she did exactly the same in the US championship as well! Her Wimbledon hat trick came in 1968, when she won the singles title for the third time, the first woman to do so for 15 years. As well as winning on the court, Billie Jean King was a strong campaigner for equal rights for women tennis players off the court. In 1971 she became the first woman tennis player to earn over $100,000 in one year.

She won the Wimbledon singles title again in 1972, 1973 and 1975. She won the women's doubles in 1961, 1962, 1965, 1968, 1970, 1971, 1972, 1973 and 1979. And she won the Australian singles once in 1968, the US singles three times in 1971, 1972 and 1974 and the French singles in 1972. She also scored several victories in the French and US doubles and mixed doubles tournaments.

Rod Laver

Rod Laver, the great Australian tennis player of the 1960's, is the only man ever to complete the grand slam as both an amateur and a professional. As a youngster Rod Laver looked far from a potential champion. Lightly-built, fairly short and slightly bandy-legged, he had to train and exercise hard to convince his coaches that he had the makings of a great player. He was picked to play for Australia in the Davis Cup in 1957. In 1960 he won the Australian title. He won Wimbledon in 1961 and 1962, the year of his amateur grand slam, in which he also won the Italian and German championships, to set a new record. After turning professional in 1963 it took him three years to find his championship form on the circuits.

In 1969 he won his professional grand slam and became the leading player in the world. He played for Australia again in the Davis Cup in 1973 and, in spite of being out of form, won all his six matches to beat Czechoslovakia in the semi-final and the U.S.A. in the final itself. His career included wins in the French, Wimbledon and Australian doubles, partnered by fellow Australian, Roy Emerson.

Ilie Nastase

Ilie Nastase is the only Rumanian player to have his name on the Wimbledon championship roll; he and Rosemary Casals won the mixed doubles title twice in 1970 and 1972. His name could easily have appeared under the list of men's singles champions were it not for his temperamental attitude which so often spoils his otherwise faultless play. In 1972 he lost the final to Stan Smith after constantly changing his racket and allowing his nerves to distract him from the game. As it was the match was hailed as one of the most exciting Wimbledon finals to that date. Four years later he again lost the final at Wimbledon, this time to Bjorn Borg. Borg's coolness on court was matched by Nastase's ability to lose concentration. After reaching the final without losing a set and after leading 3–0 in the first set against Borg, his attention seemed to wander from the game, and in spite of fighting back to 7–7 in the last set, he was eventually beaten by the ice-cool Swede.

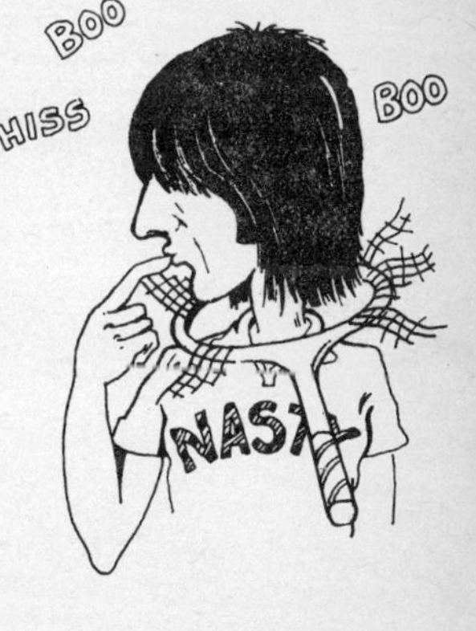

Nastase or 'Nasty' as he is sometimes called by those who disapprove of his behaviour on court has more rows and arguments with crowds and officials than almost any other player. Experts agree that if was not for his temperamental behaviour he would have won far more championship title than he already has.

However, it has to be said that it is thanks to this fiery streak that Ilie Nastase is the genius that he is at times. When he is playing at his best, Nastase is unbeatable. Dramatic, aggressive, athletic and daring he lets his near perfect technique play brilliant smashes, thunderous services and sizzling passing shots. On his good days he is the most attractive and exciting player any crowd could hope to watch. This combination of skills has enabled him to win the US championship in 1972, the French championship in 1973, the Grand Prix Masters Tournament in 1971, 1972, 1973 and 1975 and he was winner of the Grand Prix in 1972 and 1973 also.

Suzanne Lenglen

Suzanne Lenglen, the French player who was almost unbeatable from 1919 until 1926, is one of the legends of tennis. During that time she lost only one match, won the French singles title three times, Wimbledon six, the French mixed doubles seven times and the Wimbledon three times. She was the first player to draw huge crowds through the force of her personality and the exciting way in which she played. Her game was dominated by beautiful, sweeping strokes, her feet seldom seemed to touch the ground and many believe that she was the most elegant and graceful player in the history of the sport.

Virginia Wade

Without question, 1977 was the most memorable in Virginia Wade's long tennis career. Sixteen years of effort to reach the Wimbledon finals finally paid off when she became the women's singles champion in the year which marked the centenary of the tournament.

In previous attempts Virginia had reached the quarter-finals six times and the semi-finals twice, each time to be beaten. As the leading British player of recent years Virginia Wade achieved notable success by becoming the first winner of the US Open championship in 1968. During her career she has won many other tournaments and competitions, but it would be fair to say that she has not always shown the great promise that her game at its best suggests she can play. She has a strong, deep service, which many think is the most powerful among the leading women players in the world. She enjoys playing hard, attacking shots and when she is confident, her command of a game is second to none. However, she has suffered in the past from the drama of important matches, which have allowed others to gain the upper hand. Pre-match nerves combined with unexpected play from opponents have thrown her in matches and she has walked off a disappointed loser. In recent years though she has shown greater signs of relaxing on court and her game has improved accordingly.

Fred Perry

Fred Perry was the man responsible for restoring Britain's reputation as a leading tennis nation in the 1930's, so it's surprising to learn that he only took up tennis when he was 19.

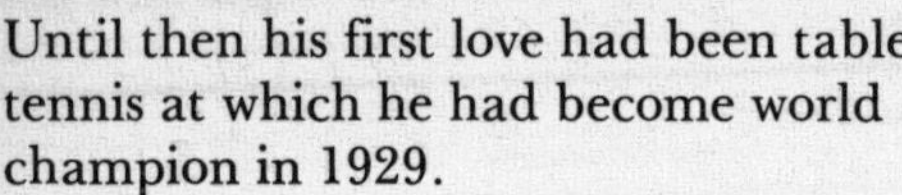

Until then his first love had been table tennis at which he had become world champion in 1929.

Fred Perry was a tireless player who never seemed to run out of energy during a match. He used a powerful whiplash action which all his opponents feared. He enjoyed playing fast attacking tennis and had a running forehand which few could return. In 1933 he was largely responsible for Britain's victory in the Davis Cup, which France had won for the previous six years. In that year he also became the first English player to win the US singles title for 30 years. Between 1934 and 1936 he won all the major championships, setting a hat trick record for Wimbledon which was only beaten by Bjorn Borg when he won the title for a fourth year in succession in 1979. He played his first Davis Cup match against Monaco in 1931 and is regarded as being one of the most successful of Davis Cup players of all time; out of the 52 rubbers he played in the Davis Cup Fred Perry won 45. As an indication of his sporting ability he once accomplished a unique feat in Paris in 1932 when he won a lawn tennis final on wood playing during the daytime, and played table tennis in the evenings eventually to win the Paris table tennis tournament. After becoming a professional Fred Perry lived in America and in recent years he has become well known as a writer and commentator on tennis.

John McEnroe

Today John McEnroe is the world's leading player, after toppling Bjorn Borg from his champion's seat. McEnroe is fiery, aggressive and forceful both in his game and in his manner on court.

He is also a supreme professional. His famous arguments with line judges are often based on his eagle-like eyes which see the bounce of the ball often with greater clarity than the judge, because McEnroe has the advantage of knowing exactly where the ball is going to bounce. He combines the athleticism of Borg with the punch and attack of Jimmy Connors. He fights and fights and does not stop fighting until the final point has been decided. In 1980 he played in a memorable final at Wimbledon against Bjorn Borg. At the start of the the match McEnroe was booed by some of the crowd after some of his unsporting behaviour in earlier rounds. However, as the epic match progressed the crowd's attitude changed to one of admiration and when he was narrowly defeated at the end they rose to applaud him as a gallant loser. The following year in a repeat final, John McEnroe proved his supremacy by finally ending Borg's run of successes. Not that this was McEnroc's only Wimbledon victory, he won the men's doubles with Peter Fleming in 1981 also, repeating their victory in the same event two years before. At home McEnroe won the US men's singles in 1979, 1980 and 1981. He was named WCT champion in 1979 and 1981. He and Peter Fleming won the Master's doubles in 1978, 1979, 1980 and 1981. And he was Grand Prix winner in 1979 and 1980 after winning the Grand Prix Masters Tournament in 1978.

Chris Lloyd

Like Jimmy Connors, Chris Lloyd, as Miss Evert, blazed a trail for young players through the tennis world of the 1970's. When she was still 16 she became the youngest player to represent the USA, playing an important part in winning the Wightman Cup; in the same year, 1971, she had 46 consecutive singles wins as well.

She won the Wimbledon women's singles for the first time in 1974, becoming the fourth youngest champion. She won that title again in 1976 and in 1981. In 1976 she also won the women's doubles at Wimbledon, partnered by Martina Navratilova. At home in the USA she won the singles title in 1975, 1976, 1977, 1978 and 1980. The French title fell to her in 1974, 1975, 1979, 1980 and 1982. And she was declared world champion by the International Tennis Federation in 1978 and 1980. Chris Lloyd is without doubt the most outstanding woman player at present. Her accuracy, her devastating two-handed backhand and her ability to remain cool in the most testing games have made her champion among champions.

USEFUL ADDRESSES

Lawn Tennis Association,
Barons Court,
West Kensington,
London W.14

Lawn Tennis Foundation (for Prudential Tennis Ladders and Nestles Ladder)
Queens Club,
Barons Court,
London,
W.14

British School L.T.A.
The Secretary,
Monksilver,
72 Boxgrove Road,
Guilford,
Surrey

Australia

Lawn Tennis Association of Australia,
P.O. Box 343,
South Yarra,
Victoria,
3141

Canada

Canadian Tennis Association,
National Sport and Recreation Centre,
333 River Road,
11th Floor,
Ottawa,
Ontario, K1L 8B9

Ireland

Irish Lawn Tennis Association,
15 Cilleanna,
Raheny,
Dublin 5

New Zealand

New Zealand Lawn Tennis Association,
P.O. Box 1645,
Wellington

U.S.A.

United States Tennis Association,
51 East 42nd Street,
New York,
New York,
10017